mustsees
Venice

Rialto/©R. Mattes/MICHELIN

mustsees **Venice**

Editorial Manager	Jonathan P. Gilbert
Principal Writer	Judy Edelhoff
Production Manager	Natasha G. George
Cartography	John Dear
Photo Editor	Yoshimi Kanazawa
Photo Researcher	Nicole D. Jordan
Proofreader	Janet McCann
Layout	Jonathan P. Gilbert, Natasha G. George
Interior Design	Chris Bell, cbdesign
Cover Design	Chris Bell, cbdesign, Natasha G. George

Contact Us	Michelin Travel and Lifestyle
	One Parkway South
	Greenville, SC 29615
	USA
	www.michelintravel.com
	michelin.guides@us.michelin.com
	Michelin TravelPartner
	Hannay House
	39 Clarendon Road
	Watford, Herts WD17 1JA
	UK
	(01923) 205 240
	www.ViaMichelin.com
	travelpubsales@uk.michelin.com

Special Sales	For information regarding bulk sales, customized editions and premium sales, please contact our Customer Service Departments:
	USA 1-800-432-6277
	UK (01923) 205 240
	Canada 1-800-361-8236

Michelin Apa Publications Ltd

58 Borough High Street, London SE1 1XF, United Kingdom

© 2012 Michelin Apa Publications Ltd
ISBN 978-1-907099-71-7
Printed: December 2011
Printed and bound: Himmer, Germany

Note to the reader:

While every effort is made to ensure that all information printed in this guide is correct and up-to-date, Michelin Apa Publications Ltd. accepts no liability for any direct, indirect or consequential losses howsoever caused so far as such can be excluded by law. Admission prices listed for sights in this guide are for a single adult, unless otherwise specified.

Welcome to Venice

©Image Source/Photononstop

Grand Canal

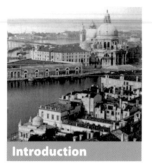

p 76

TABLE OF CONTENTS

★★★ATTRACTIONS

Unmissable attractions awarded three stars in this guide include:

Piazza San Marco p 24

©Videocomunicazione Città di Venezia

Grand Canal p 20

©G. Glinsk/Fotolia.co

Rialto Bridge p 21, p 35

©Videocomunicazione Città di Venezia

I MUST KNOW

Santa Maria Gloriosa dei Frari   p 74

©S. Lubenow/Look/Photononstop

Rialto area   p 35

©marion pietz/age fotostock

Detail, Basilica di San Marco   p 26

©Y. Talensac/Photononstop

★★★ ATTRACTIONS

Unmissable sights in and around Vegas

For more than 75 years people have used the Michelin stars to take the guesswork out of travel. Our star-rating system helps you make the best decision on where to go, what to do, and what to see.

★★★	Unmissable
★★	Worth a trip
★	Worth a detour
No star	Recommended

MUST KNOW

 # ACTIVITIES

Unmissable Venice events, shows, restaurants and more

For every gondola ride and canal-side dinner there are a thousand more activities. We recommend every activity in this guide, but our top picks are highlighted with the Michelin Man logo. *Look-out for the Michelin Man throughout the guide for the top activities.*

CALENDAR OF EVENTS

Venice plays host to some important and colourful annual events. Please note that dates may change from year to year. *For more detailed information, contact Turismo Venezia (www.turismovenezia.it).*

6 January

Regata della Befana – Epiphany boat race with contestants dressed as witches racing to a giant stocking at Rialto Bridge!

10 days before Lent (Feb–Mar)

Carnival – The year's most famous celebration features costumed revellers in masks throughout the city (*see Must Do*).

March

Su e zo per i ponti – A race through the streets and over the bridges of Venice.

Maundy Thursday

Benediction – Candle-lighting procession outside Basilica di San Marco.

25 April

Feast day of St Mark – Men give their sweethearts a *bòcolo* (a red rose), gondolas race between Punta della Dogana, and Venetians eat *risi e bisi*.

May

1 May – Cavillino hosts **Festa della Sparesea** (new asparagus) with a regatta.
The **Vogalonga** – A non-competitive regatta open to foreign rowers around the islands. www.vogalonga.com.

Ascension Day (Sunday after)

La Sens commemorates the Sposalizio del Mar, the Doge's ritual marriage with the sea. The "groom" now is a city official. A week later, **Vogalonga a Sens** (the long row) is a 32km/20mi race from San Marco to Burano and back.

Vogalonga

©Vogalonga/ Axel Fassio

July: Festa del Redentore

©Venezia Marketing ed Eventi

June

Biennale – *Even-numbered years only. Jun–Nov (Dance in Jun; Theatre end of Jul)*. International exhibitions of art and culture (*see Sant'Elena e San Pietro and Must Do*).

The **Heineken Jammin Festival** takes place at San Giuliano Park, in Mestre on the mainland. The 2010 line-up included the Cranberries, 30 Seconds to Mars, Black Eyed Peas, Pearl Jam and Massive Attack, while 2011 brought Coldplay to the event.

The **Regatta dei Santi Giovanni e Paolo** is a boat race for young people (under 25 years of age), from Murano toward Fondamenta Nuove to the Ponte Mendicanti near Campo Santi Giovanni e Paolo.

Third Sunday in July

Festa del Redentore – The Feast of the Redeemer commemorates the end of the plague in 1576. Boats link to form a platform so that worshippers can walk across the Giudecca Canal. The night before, a crowd assembles along the Zattere to watch fireworks (*see Giudecca*).

Late August–early Sept

Venice Film Festival – This glittering movie jamboree sees top stars and emerging talent from all over the world jetting over to the Lido to watch movies and talk cinema (*see Il Lido*).

September

Regata Storica – *First Sun in Sept.* An historic regatta re-enactment with a costumed pageant and gondola, as well as boat races in historical costume on the Grand Canal.

Festival Galuppi – *Sept–Oct* 18C music performed in historic churches, palaces and theatres.

21 November

Feast of the Madonna della Salute – This feast commemorates the end of the plague in 1576 with a bridge of boats across the Grand Canal to La Salute (*see La Salute*).

PRACTICAL INFORMATION

WHEN TO GO

Venice is glorious year-round. **Spring** and **autumn** weather is ideal, attracting crowds. Tourism tapers off in early December, January and August. **Carnevale**, a moveable and highly colourful feast, leads up to Lent.

Book hotels (and restaurants) months in advance.

Summer, hot and humid, is graced with sea breezes best enjoyed on the outer islands. Verify that rooms have AC. Mosquito repellent is handy for campers. Crowds are intense in peak periods, so explore lesser-known areas and islands. Cool off with a sailing tour or lesson, or join the crowds at the Lido beaches. October–December are the wettest months.

Winter brings silvery overcast skies, some say the best time to see Venice. Atmospheric mists and fogs, and *acqua alta* (floods) blend melancholy, mystery and beauty with less crowded sights. Cold and clinging damp can be uncomfortable, so dress in layers and bring high rain boots. Visitor hours may be reduced; some places close. Crisp, clear days bring views of the mountains beyond the lagoon. Christmas is magical with churches festively decorated, bringing back the crowds until early January, the brief calm before Carnevale.

Wellington boots

Curious and highly memorable is the sight of *acqua alta* (high water) flooding the streets of Venice. The more flood-prone streets and squares are criss-crossed with wooden walkways. The city, usually so stylish, sees Venetians and visitors alike wearing ungainly wellingtons, plastic boots and even plastic bags wrapped around their feet in an effort to keep dry. In hand will be a chic shoe bag, so the transformation from ungainly duckling to swan is complete for the opera, concert or dinner.

KNOW BEFORE YOU GO
Useful Websites

www.turismovenezia.it – Attractions in Venice, the city and its province.
www.comune.venezia.it Venice's town council puts out locals news, interesting, too, for visitors. Don't miss the FAQ page.
www.veniceworld.com – Hotels, dining, transportation, events.
www.hellovenezia.com – Transport details, events, tourist passes.
www.gondolavenezia.it – The gondola and everything about it.

Visitor Information
Italian National Tourist Board
www.enit.it.
UK – 1, Princes Street, London W1B 2AY. 020 7408 1254.
USA – New York: 630, Fifth Avenue - Suite 1565. 212 2455618.
Los Angeles: 12400 Wilshire Blvd. - Suite 550. 310 820-1898.
Chicago: 500 N. Michigan Avenue Suite 506. 312 644-0996.
Canada – 110 Yonge Street, Suite 503, Toronto M5C 1T4. 416 925-4882.

Guided Tours

Tours of the city offer visitors a guided walking tour with the option of a gondola ride. If you do hanker to ride in the city's most famous mode of transport, this is cheaper than booking a private gondola ride. In a city that requires constant map-checking, a tour can be a good way to optimize your time. Select unusual themes: "Spicy Venice" meanders through the Rialto area, listening to the conquests of Casanova and of libertine Venice in the 18C; and "Venetian Legends" tours the districts of Castello and Cannaregio to discover the 'dark' side of Venetian tradition. Book tours at the tourist office – wear comfortable walking shoes!

Tourist Offices in Venice

The **Azienda Promozione Turismo (APT)** will help you find accommodation and sights, and sells tourist maps.

Venice Pavilion (*041 529 87 11, www.turismovenezia.it*), near the Giardini Reali and St. Mark's Square, offers tourist information, plus travel books and novels on Venice in several languages.

Other tourist offices: **Procuratie Nuove**, off Piazza San Marco; **Piazzale Roma** (*Garage San Marco*); and Santa Lucia Railway Station. Also at **Lido** (*Gran Viale, 041 529 87 11, open Jun–Sept only*) and **Marco Polo Airport** (*041 541 5133*).

International Visitors

Italian Embassies abroad

UK – London, www.embitaly.org.uk.
USA – Washington, DC, www.italyemb.org.
Canada – Ottowa, www.ambottawa.esteri.it.

Italian Consulates Abroad

UK – London, www.embitaly.org.uk.
Edinburgh, www.consedimburgo.esteri.it.
USA – New York, www.cons newyork.esteri.it.
Canada – Montreal, Toronto, www.constoronto.esteri.it.

Foreign Embassies and Consulates in Italy

Australia – **Consulate:** Via della Liberta' 12, Venice. 041 5093061.
Embassy: Via Antonio Bosio 5, Rome. 06 85 27 21. www.italy.embassy.gov.au.

Canada – **Consulate:** Riviera Ruvvante 25, Padova. 049 87 64 833.
Embassy: Via Salaria 243, Rome. 06 85 44 41.

Ireland – For consulate see UK below. www.ambasciata-irlanda.it.
Embassy: Piazza di Campitelli 3, Rome. 06 69 79 121.

UK – Honorary consulate in Venice: Piazzale Donatori di Sangue 2/5, Mestre. 041 5055 990.
British embassy: Via XX Settembre 80a, Rome. 06 42 20 00 01.

USA – Consular agent at Marco Polo Airport. **Consulate:** Via Principe Amedeo 2/10, Milan. 02 290 351.
Embassy: Via Veneto 119a, Rome. 06 46 741. www.usembassy.it.

Entry Requirements

No visas are required for stays of less than 90 days for Australian, New Zealand, Canadian and US citizens. Travellers to Italy must be in possession of a valid national passport. Citizens of other European Union countries need only a national identity card (or passport if you are form the UK).

In case of loss or theft report to the embassy or consulate and to the local police.

Customs Regulations
For the regulations on import, export and duty-free allowances, US citizens should consult *www.customs.gov*.
British citizens consult *www.hmce. gov.uk* (enter "Travel" option).

Health
US visitors should verify whether their policies cover overseas health care and emergencies. If not, it's wise to purchase optional cover. British subjects should obtain a **European Health Insurance Card (EHIC)**, available from main post offices, before leaving home. However, cover is minimal; separate travel and medical insurance is highly recommended.

Accessibility
Many Venetian historic monuments and attractions do not have elevators or wheelchair facilities, although some motorised ramps and lifts have been installed on some of its many bridges. Wheelchairs can be loaded onto the *vaporetti* but not onto the gondolas. Some water taxis are specially equipped.
www2.comune.venezia.it/handicap has accessibility information; www.comune.venezia.it/ letturagevolata, in Italian, has useful information for the visually impaired.
Tourism for All UK (formerly Holiday Care), *0845 124 9971. www.tourismforall.org.uk*).
RADAR (Royal Association for Disability and Rehabilitation), 12 City Forum, 250 City Road,

London EC1V 8AF. *020 7250 3222. www.radar.org.uk*.
Society for Accessible Travel & Hospitality – *www.sath.org*.
Accessible Venice tips at *www. tour-web.com/accessibleitaly/ infovene.htm*.

GETTING THERE
By Air
Marco Polo Airport
(*www.veniceairport.it*) is served by major European carriers, by Delta, and by budget airlines including easyJet. Treviso's Antonio Canova airport (*www.trevisoairport.it*), 30km/18mi north of Venice, is served by several budget airlines including Ryanair.

Airport Transfers
By Bus: Marco Polo airport is linked to Venice's Piazzale Roma by **ACTV Bus** 35 (€5. *www.actv.it*). From Treviso airport ATVO buses run to Mestre railway station and Venice (Piazzale Roma). The journey takes around 1hr 10min.
By Taxi: Taxis are available from Marco Polo to Piazzale Roma (about €33).
By Water: Alilaguna
(*www.alilaguna.it*) boats cross the lagoon; the Red Line, the Blue Line and the Orange Line serve all major parts of the city, including the Lido and Murano. The dock for Alilaguna (and private water taxis) is a 5-minute walk from the airport, or a 1-minute ride on the airport shuttle (€1). The ride takes about 70 minutes. Consult the website for timetables and prices.
Private **water taxis** offer a much faster 35-minute door-to-door service, but are very expensive (expect to pay at least €100).

By Ship

Venice Ferry Port is the busiest and most popular Southern European entrance to the Adriatic and Mediterranean Sea.

Venezia Lines (*www.venezia lines.com*) operates from Venice to Slovenia and Croatia, with cruises from two to five hours.

Viamare (www.viamare.com) runs ferries between Venice and Rabac.

Anek Lines and **Minoan Lines** (*www.minoan.gr*) operate ferries from Venice to Patras and Igoumenitsa on the Greek mainland, and also to Corfu.

Ferry booking services: *www.directferries.co.uk, or www.aferry.co.uk*.

Cruise operators generally use the main Marittima terminal, or sometimes dock along the Zattere along the Giudecca Canal, a vaporetto ride or an easy walk away (get details before disembarking).

By Train

Trenitalia (www.trenitalia.com) services Venice from various Italian cities with speedier service on the Eurostar, slower but more economical service on regional trains, and overnight sleeping cars from some destinations.

Venice Simplon-Orient-Express Ltd operates the famous, luxurious midnight blue train, beautifully restored 1920s and '30s carriages (departs London with stops in Paris, Innsbruck, Verona and Venice). It's expensive, but some discounts apply between late autumn and early spring.

Thomas Cook European Rail Timetable gives Europe rail timetables. Also check **Rail Europe** (*www.raileurope.co.uk*) and **Italian State Railways** (*www.trenitaliaplus.com*).

By Coach/Bus

National Express/Eurolines. *08717 818 181. www.eurolines. co.uk*. Coach services from Victoria Coach Station, London.

By Car

Formalities

Nationals of the European Union require a valid **national driving licence**. US citizens should obtain an **international driver's license** from the American Automobile Association (*www.aaa.com*). The driver must have the vehicle's current **registration document** and a **green card** for insurance.

Main roads

Venice is situated off the A 4 Torino–Trieste road, reached from the south by the A 13 Bologna–Padua road. Exit at Mestre onto the SS 11, then cross the Ponte della Libertà to Piazzale Roma or park at Tronchetto.

Orient-Express

The luxurious time-warp that is the Venice Simplon-Orient-Express, launched in 1982, leaves from London for Venice on Thursdays and Sundays, stopping in Paris, Innsbruck and Verona. The full trip takes about 32hr, covering 1 715km/1 065mi. **Venice Simplon-Orient-Express Ltd.** in the UK: 44 (0) 20 7921 4007, or in North America 1 401 351 7518; www.orient-express.com.

PRACTICAL INFORMATION

Maps

Michelin Tourist and Motoring Atlas Italy and Michelin Maps *no. 705* Europe (1:3 000 000), *no. 735* Italy (1:1 000 000) and *no. 562* Northeast Italy (1:400 000) will make route planning easier.

Parking

Piazzale Roma – ASM garage (*041 27 27 211. www.asmvenezia.it*) at Piazzale Roma charges a daily rate of €24.

Garage San Marco (*041 52 32 213. www.garagesanmarco.it*) at Piazzale Roma charges €22 for 12hr and €28 for 24hr.

Tronchetto – To the west of Piazzale Roma, Interparking Italia (*041 52 07 555. www.venice parking.it*) on the island of Tronchetto – exit from the Liberty Bridge, serviced by ferry and vaporetto – charges cars, camper-vans and caravans around €20 for 24hr. There is also a ferry service for vehicles to the Lido.

On Foot

The easiest way of getting around is on foot. Carry a good, detailed city map but don't worry if you get lost – you may find yourself away from the crowds with rare glimpses of Venetians.

Venice's address numbers on homes and business can reach high digits (up to almost 7 000), which refer to an individual address within the **sestiere** rather than to a particular street or square. Numbers on one side of the street may have little relation to those on the opposite.

Yellow signs with directional arrows point to major sights like the Rialto and Piazza San Marco.

On Water

Venice has one of the world's most remarkable and efficient transportation systems. Try to experience all variations.

Vaporetto (Waterbus)

See map of vaporetto routes.
The vaporetto (waterbus) is to Venice what buses are to ordinary cities. **ACTV** (*041 27 22 111. www.actv.it*) operates the lumbering *vaporetto* (plural, *vaporetti*), and, for longer distances, the faster *motoscafo* (motor boat, plural *motoscafi*). The name of a *vaporetto* stop indicates the vicinity in which the waterbus will stop. Traffic on the Grand Canal is often congested and services may sometimes be erratic. Night service is reduced, with timetables. Single **tickets** may be purchased from kiosks or machines at landings, from Hellovenezia ticket desks, and from shops displaying the ACTV sign. Best value is a travel card, available in increments from 24, 48 and 72 hours, as well as for 7 days. A single ticket is €6.50 (or €1.30/75 min. with **Hello Venezia** card) and allows 1hr of travel, but *not* a return trip. A three-day "youth card" is available: enquire at the Hellovenezia ticket desks. If you board without a ticket, you must request one immediately from the *marinaio* (sailor/attendant), otherwise you may be fined.

Line 1 runs from Piazzale Roma and Ferrovia (railway station), the full length of the Grand Canal, to Rialto, Piazza San Marco and the Lido. This is faster, making only these stops.

Line 2, like Line 1, also follows the Grand Canal, but makes 13 stops adding Giudecca, Accademia and others.

Lines 41 and 42 go further out to Murano, and, by request, Certosa. **Line 51** makes a counterclockwise circular route from the Lido around Venice, while **Line 52** runs clockwise. ACTV has complete information.

Water Taxis

Beware of unauthorized boats that overcharge the unsuspecting visitor! Use motor launches with a yellow registration number plate inscribed with the symbol of Venice on the boarding side.

Note that the meter is clearly visible and that charge rates are displayed. The fixed starting price is €13 then a charge of €1.80 per minute. A ten-minute ride across the city centre will cost approximately €30 (with small additional charges for luggage and if the number of passengers exceeds four). For queries or complaints, contact Azienda Trasporto Persone Venezia, S. Polo, 618/a. 041 5210506.

Self Drive Boats

Recommended only for experienced boaters. This unusual and exciting way to explore the city requires skill to navigate busy Venetian lagoons and canals.

A Venetian *topo* (open-topped motorboat) accommodates up to six people and can be rented from two operators:

Brussa (*041 715787, brussaisboat.it*) by the Ponte delle Guglie, near the station. €20 per hour.

Cantiere Lizzio/Sport e Lavoro, 2606 Cannaregio (*041 721 055*). €120 for a day.

Gondolas

For a relaxing trip on a gondola, put your hand in your wallet: 40min along the canals during the daytime will cost you, and up to 5 other passengers, €80 (a musical serenade is extra). Every additional 20min will be charged an extra €40. A 40min trip by gondola at night (7pm–8am) costs €100, with an extra €50 for every additional 20min. These are the official charges, but may be subject to negotiation. You can request the gondolier to follow the route you prefer.

Istituzione per la Conservazione della Gondola e la Tutela del Gondoliere (*041 52 85 075, www.gondolavenezia.it/storia_tariffe.asp*) has further information.

Traghetti

A budget gondola ride is to be had on a *traghetto* (gondola ferry) at eight points along the Grand Canal (Ferrovia, San Marcuola, Santa Sofia, Riva del Carbon, San Tomà, San Samuele, Santa Maria del Giglio and Dogana). The relative absence of bridges across the Grand Canal (Costituzione, Scalzi, Rialto and Accademia) has ensured the traditional role of gondolier to ferry passengers, despite the prevalence of the *vaporetto*. The Venetian custom is to stand during the brief crossing, although unsteady passengers are better seated than fished out of the Grand Canal! A *traghetto* costs a mere €0.50 (slightly higher from San Samuele during exhibitions at Palazzo Grassi). Schedules are posted at landings, though beware they finish quite early (before 8pm) and in winter services may be suspended.

BASIC INFORMATION
Business Hours

Shops – Shops are generally open from 9am–12.30/1pm and 4pm–6pm, although many stay open during lunchtime. More shops are open in high season than in low season, and normally extend their business hours to accommodate the extra customers. Some businesses are closed on Mondays. *For bank opening times, see Money.*

Museums and Churches – The main churches in Venice are open 7am–noon and 4–6pm. Dress appropriately: long trousers for men; no bare shoulders or very short skirts for women. Coins are useful to activate lights. Museum times and days vary considerably; some also close on Mondays.

Communications

Compania Italiana Telecom (CIT) runs public telephones where customers pay at the end of the call (*Fondaco dei Tedeschi*). Reduced rates for national calls apply after 6.30pm and between 10pm and 8am for international calls.

Public phones – Public telephones are found along streets and in some bars. Use a phone card (*see below*) or telephone credit cards. Lift the receiver, insert payment, await a tone, enter the required number and wait for a reply.

Phone cards are sold in denominations of €1, €2.50, €5 and €8 and are supplied by CIT offices, post offices and tobacconists (*tabaccaio* sign has a white T on black background).

City codes – For calls within Venice, include the 041 prefix code for Venice.

For calls within Italy, enter the code for the town or district beginning with a 0, followed by the number. For international calls, enter 00 followed by the country code: 61 for Australia, 1 for Canada, 64 for New Zealand, 44 for the UK, 1 for the USA. The international code for Italy is 39, the code for Venice is 041. Note that in Italy, a "0" is the first digit of the area or city code.

Internet – Most good hotels (of 3-star status and above) provide internet access to guests. There are some internet cafés, and in 2011 the city installed a programme that offers wi-fi access in many areas.

Electricity

Voltage is 220 AC, 50 cycles per second; the sockets are for two-pin plugs. Bring an adaptor for hair dryers, shavers, computers and other electrical equipment.

Emergencies

Emergency Services 112.

Mail

Post offices are open 8.30am–2pm (noon Sat and last day of the month). The main post offices are at Fondaco dei Tedeschi and just off Piazza San Marco, behind the Napoleon Wing by the Correr museum. Letters sent **poste restante** (*fermo posta*) can be collected from the main post office. Stamps (*francobolli*) are sold in post offices and tobacconists (*tabaccheria*).

Money

The **euro** is issued in notes (€5, €10, €20, €50, €100, €200 and €500) and coins (1 cent, 2 cents, 5 cents, 10 cents, 20 cents, 50 cents, €1 and €2).

Banks – ATMs (*bancomat*) are plentiful in Venice. Banks are usually open Monday to Friday,

8.30am–1.30pm and 2.30pm–4pm. Some hotels will change travellers' cheques. Money can be changed in post offices, exchanges, trains stations and airports. Commission is always charged. Money withdrawn from *bancomat* machines has a lower commission than from bank tellers.

Credit cards – can be used at most shops, hotels and restaurants, and some petrol stations.

Pharmacies

A pharmacy (*farmacia*) is identified by a red and white or green cross. When closed, it posts the names of the nearest pharmacies that are open, as well as night pharmacies (www.farmacistivenezia.it).

Reduced Rates

If you plan on visiting the interiors of Venice's more important churches, purchase a pass from **Chorus** (www.chorusvenezia. org) at any of its 16 churches, valid for one year, and costing €9. Otherwise, admission to each of the 16 Chorus churches is €3. **Museum Pass** (*041 52 09070; www.museicivicveneziani.it, €18, valid 6 months*) offers entry to all civic museums.

Hello Venezia Card (www. hellovenezia.com) discounts a number of sights, transport, public toilets, car parks etc. A variation, Venice Card (Transport & Culture), offers unlimited public transport on land and water, free admission to 12 museums (including the Doge's Palace), and the 16 Chorus-group churches, plus discounts on other admissions to exhibitions and events. Another option is a transport-only version. Both cards are available for 3 days and 7 days.

The 3 day Venice Card (Transport & Culture) is €59 (or €82 if you choose Alilaguna boat service), and you can buy the ticket from a Hello Venezia vendor. However, online the price is cheaper: a €59 ticket, for example, costs €46.10. Average daily savings are about €25, plus you can bypass queues. "Juniors" (aged 5–29) receive special discounts.

Youth Discounts – **Rolling Venice** card (www.hellovenezia.com, €4) – young people aged 15–29 receive over 200 discounts at participating youth hostels, campsites, hotels, restaurants, museums, shops, public transport and the International Biennale of Art. Find them at tourist offices and Hello Venezia outlets.

Smoking

Smoking is officially banned in all public places, though some bars and cafés may have areas where it is possible to smoke.

Time

The time in Italy is the same as in the rest of mainland Europe (one hour ahead of the United Kingdom). Time changes during the last weekend in March and October, from summer time (*ora legale*) to winter time (*ora solare*).

Tipping

Tipping in Venice is like other European tourist-oriented cities. Restaurants often add a 12 percent service charge and *coperto* (cover charge for bread, pretzels etc) to the bill, in which case there is no need to tip further. Guides and taxi drivers will expect a tip of around 10 percent, though this is by no means compulsory. Porters, hotel maids and toilet attendants should be tipped a few coins.

LA SERENISSIMA

La Serenissima sits on the lagoon, profoundly entwined with the sea. Forever fragile, her future is anything but assured, as the nature that provides her means of communication, transport and trade threatens to entomb her. The world's most romantic city sheds her melancholy cares to put on grand masquerades and festivals, to banter in intimate wine bars (baccari), host orchestras in grand squares, and lavish decadence on interiors, art, palaces, textiles, wine and food. All the while Venice illuminates with her refinement, treasures and gaiety. As Lord Byron once said, Venice is "a fairy city of the heart".

Floating Mirage

Water is the key to understanding, exploring, and enjoying Venice. No visit, even for a day, should omit a glimpse of the Adriatic Sea, from where Venice commanded her empire and traders amassed their wealth. Nature and artifice combine magically in a city built atop 117 islands interconnected by the sea, lagoon, rivers, and canals. Bridges, belltowers, churches, lighthouses and palaces adorn every available piece of land. This delicate beauty flexes a lot of muscle: the skyline reveals factories and shipbuilding, while fishermen haul their catches. The loading and unloading from boats is continual – from cargo to people – pulling in and pushing off, navigating busy channels and narrow canals. The simplest of daily tasks take on new fascination in this island city. You will need to allow at the very least four to five days to scratch the surface of all six sestieri – the six central neighbourhoods – plus the other islands.

Beyond the sestieri you will see glassblowers mould their craft with flames, restorers repair antique boats, sailors show the ropes to novices and lacemakers show their intricate patterns. Swim and relax at Art Nouveau beach resorts, hike around a nature preserve, see spindly fishing wharves, marvel at fanciful mosaics, and visit spiritual retreats. Such splendours take time to explore and are well worth all of the days that you can dedicate.

Venice Canals and the
Santa Maria Della Salute, 1870s

©Corbis

Transport is essential. Don't just watch the parade of boats; hop aboard. Experience the sea, the lagoon, the canals. A gondola ride is a must: luxuriate for as much time as your wallet commands; or take a traghetto across the Grand Canal, over in a few minutes but it's a thrill nevertheless.

Venice rose along with the success of its merchant class, so be prepared for an onslaught of beautiful **design and crafts**. Venice shopping is a particular delight due to the city's many active artisans, who practice trades that are hard to find elsewhere. Look for mask makers skilled in papier mâché, bookbinders, costume designers, goldsmiths, paper marblers, weavers and their artisanal textiles, or update your wardrobe with a made-to-measure shirt. Don't expect bargains, seek quality.

A Bit of History

The **birth of Venice** was relatively late compared to those of Rome and Florence; long after the Latins, Etruscans, and Romans had lost their empires. Venice began in the early **Middle Ages** as a safe haven on stilts built by refugees who fled barbarian attacks. In the 5C Attila the Hun invaded Torcello. Later, Lombards swept through terra firma, launching widespread migration to the lagoon islands. By 726 Venice had its first documented **Doge**, Orso Ipato. By 774, Venice requested Charlemagne's assistance to push out the Lombards.

Venetian merchants are credited with stealing the remains of **St. Mark** from Alexandria, Egypt in 828, with the first basilica completed around 832. Having rid the nearby sea of pirates, in the year 1000 Pietro Orseolo celebrated Venice's first marriage to the sea. By the **First Crusade** in 1095, Venice was a major point of departure, supply, and arrival for knights, pilgrims, sailors and merchants. In 1171, the six sestieri (districts) of Venice were designated and the first bridge, the Rialto, was constructed two years later. Venice conquered Constantinople in 1204, which brought an abundance of riches. By the end of that century Marco Polo would depart on his famous journey to China. Venice maintained an impressive reign over the sea, but the next century brought a devastating enemy that decimated the population; the bubonic **plague**. It would strike again in the 16C and 17C.

Renaissance Venice had its own 15C genius in Giovanni Bellini and Titian, followed by architect Andrea Palladio, and painters Tintoretto and Veronese, to name just a few. In the 16–18C, Venice held onto its reputation for luxury, sophistication, and pleasure.

Napoleon's 1797 invasion brought the Venetian Republic to an end and the exit of the final doge. But the French were soon driven out, in 1815, by the Austrians. In the 19C Venice became a highlight for the **Romantic** poets and a must on the Grand Tour.

In the 19C the Biennale was launched, followed in the 20C by the Film Festival. Having left its most decadent days of **Carnevale** back in the 18C, the 1979 revival of the festival brought a surge of international pleasure-seeking visitors that continues to this day. Venice's allure remains.

GRAND CANAL★★★

Arguably the most famous, the most beautiful and certainly the most unusual main boulevard in the world, the Grand Canal bisects the island of Venice as an inverted S. When he was living in Palazzo Mocenigo, Lord Byron was in the habit of swimming across the Grand Canal. Mark Twain described the appearance of the canal in moonlight as magical; Goethe felt himself to be "Lord of the Adriatic" here; and Dickens, convinced the ghost of Shylock roamed the bridges of the city, felt the spirit of Shakespeare strongly in Venice. Artists from Canaletto to Sargent have painted the Canal, from sublime tranquil moments to chaotic traffic jams and battles. A short journey along the canal will undoubtedly leave as magical an impression on modern-day travellers as it did on its illustrious visitors of the past. It is only 3km/2mi long, though packs so much in that it feels much bigger.

A Bit of History

The origins of the Grand Canal, which may once have been a branch of the River Medoacus, are lost in time. The *traghetti* (gondolas which cross the river) have provided a ferry service between the banks of the canal since the year 1000. Some of the existing landing stages have been in place since the 13C, many either serving mills that were operated by the tides, or *squeri* where the gondolas were built. Then there were the workshops for the Guild of Wool Weavers and Clothmakers, which employed the poor to card, finish, dye and press textiles.

Along the canal the beauty of the city unfolds: façades of vibrant colours, resplendent with gilding, exude the festive spirit and optimism of the Venetians, who have kept their city open, even in the Middle Ages, when the rest of the world built fortresses for defence. The *palazzi* that flank the Grand Canal are the Venetian nobility's expression of pride and self-satisfaction: only they could acquire a tract of this water garden (*see Il Ghetto: Palazzo*

Labia). Commercial, banking and state enterprises have been in operation along the canal since the Renaissance; churches and *palazzi* were constructed right up until the Republic had its last gasp.

Highlights
Left Bank

At the death of Baldassare Longhena (1682), completion of **Ca' Pesaro★** was assigned to Antonio Gaspari (c.1670–c.1730). Today, the building is home to the Museum of Oriental Art and the International Gallery of Modern Art (*see Rialto*).

Further on the glorious façade of **Ca' Foscari★** rises above the Grand Canal at the junction with the Rio Foscari. Perfect symmetry aligns the three orders of arched windows that alternate with single light openings and stonework. Nowadays it is part of the university (*see I Carmini*).

Ca' Rezzonico★★ was the last palace designed by Longhena, who lived to see only the completion of the first floor, before Massari took over. Today it is home to the Museo del '700 veneziano, or Museum

MUST SEE

Seeing the Canal

To best experience the Grand Canal, take the *vaporetto* from the railway station (Santa Lucia) to Piazza San Marco. Choose a *vaporetto* with open-air seating in front or back for the best views. Seats are few and in great demand, but riders come and go. The ride, 35–40min non-stop, departs from Santa Lucia (Ferrovia Scalzi) and chugs to Piazza San Marco, but you could spend days hopping on or off at places of interest. If you can get a seat, it makes a perfect break from walking across bridges, up steps and through back alleys thronged with visitors.

of 18C Venice (*see I Carmini*), and collections of Venetian finery related to the Carnival. The next stop is the **Accademia★★★** (Academy of Fine Arts), which has been housed here since the beginning of the 19C (*see Accademia*).

The Palazzo Venier dei Leoni currently houses the world-famous **Peggy Guggenheim Collection★★** of modern art (*see La Salute*). Nearby, **Ca' Dario★** is a small late-15C palazzo recognisable by its colourful marble decoration. It was built by the Lombardo family for Giovanni Dario, the secretary to the Senate of the Republic at the Sultan's court.

Beyond, the massive white structure of the **Santa Maria della Salute★★**, with its distinctive spiral volutes (the so-called *orecchioni* or big ears), is visible from afar. Designed by Longhena, it was erected upon the wishes of the doge as a gesture of supplication to end the plague of 1630 (*see La Salute*).

Right Bank

If you arrive by train at Santa Lucia, your visit begins on the Right Bank. Slightly set back from the Grand Canal is the elegant 18C **Palazzo Labia★★** on the corner of the Cannaregio Canal. Eagles protrude

from under the roof, symbol of the Labia family (*see Il Ghetto*). Not much further on, the Renaissance **Palazzo Vendramin Calergi★** (*www.vendramincalergi.com*) was commissioned by the noble family of Loredan al Codussi, who worked here from 1502 to 1504, magnificently blending Byzantine and Gothic architecture.

From 1844 it was home to the Duchesse de Berry, daughter-in-law of Charles X of France. Richard Wagner lived here and composed the second act of *Tristan and Isolde* 1858–59. In winter gamblers stake their bets here at the municipal Casino.

Further on, **Ca' d'Oro★★★** has an ornate Gothic façade, presenting a colonnade lapped by the water's edge (*see Ca' D'oro*).

The **Rialto Bridge★★★** is the most important crossing between the two banks. Since 1175 there have been six versions; the current bridge is the work of Antonio da Ponte, opened in 1591. The arcaded shops were originally used by money changers, bankers and moneylenders (*see Rialto*).

The **Palazzo Grassi★** was erected in 1749 by Giorgio Massari; it was the last Venetian palace to be built before the fall of the Republic. Today the building houses exhibitions (*www.palazzograssi.it*).

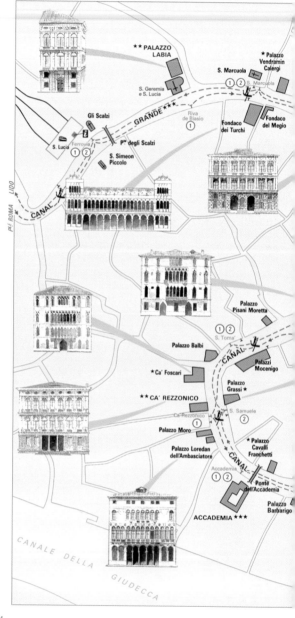

** PALAZZO LABIA

* Palazzo Vendramin Calergi

S. Marcuola

S. Geremia e S. Lucia

① ② S. Marcuola

Gli Scalzi

GRANDE ***

Riva de Biasio ①

Fondaco dei Turchi

Fondaco del Megio

S. Lucia

Ferrovia ① ②

Pⁿ degli Scalzi

S. Simeon Piccolo

PER ROMA LIDO

CANAL

Palazzo Pisani Moretta

① ② S. Toma'

Palazzo Balbi

CANAL

Palazzi Mocenigo

* Ca' Foscari

Palazzo Grassi *

** CA' REZZONICO

Ca' Rezzonico ①

S. Samuele ②

Palazzo Moro

* Palazzo Cavalli Franchetti

Palazzo Loredan dell'Ambasciatore

CANAL

Accademia ① ②

Ponte dell'Accademia

Palazzo Barbarigo

ACCADEMIA ***

CANALE DELLA GIUDECCA

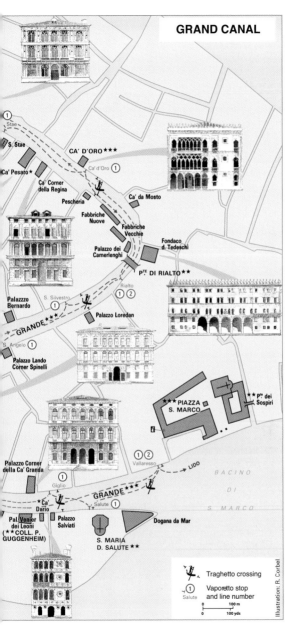

GRAND CANAL

S. Stae ①

CA' D'ORO ★★★

Ca' Pesaro ★

Ca' d'Oro ①

Ca' Corner
della Regina

Ca' da Mosto

Pescheria

Fabbriche
Nuove

Fabbriche
Vecchie

Fondaco
d. Tedeschi

Palazzo dei
Camerlenghi

Pᵀᴱ DI RIALTO ★★

Rialto
① ②

Palazzzo
Bernardo

S. Silvestro
①

GRANDE ★★★

Palazzo Loredan

S. Angelo ①

Palazzo Lando
Corner Spinelli

★★★ PIAZZA
S. MARCO

★★ Pᵗᵉ dei
Sospiri

Palazzo Corner
della Ca' Granda

① ②
Vallaresso
LIDO

BACINO

① Giglio

DI

GRANDE ★★★

★ Ca'
Dario

S MARCO

Salute ①

Pal. Venier
dei Leoni
(★★ COLL. P.
GUGGENHEIM)

Palazzo
Salviati

Dogana da Mar

S. MARIA
D. SALUTE ★★

🚣 Traghetto crossing

①
Salute
Vaporetto stop
and line number

0   100 m
0   100 yds

GRAND CANAL

PIAZZA SAN MARCO★★★

"The finest drawing room in Europe" according to Napoleon, St Mark's Square is the daily destination for tens of thousands of visitors. Beyond the onion dome, glittering mosaics and columns of St Mark and St Theodore, the gondolas and *vaporetti* come and go, pigeons flap, noisy crowds gather around the souvenir stalls, puddles mysteriously appear then vanish, and orchestras play to the habitués of the legendary cafés. Tourists follow their tour guide's raised umbrella into the basilica or loiter under the porticoes, bewitched by windows of sparkling jewellery and glass. Since time immemorial, the passing of the hours has been ceremoniously sounded by the Moors on the clock tower and the mighty bells of the campanile.

A Bit of History

A canal once ran in front of the basilica but by covering it over in 1160, the length of the piazza was tripled. The columns of St Mark and St Theodore were erected in the piazzetta, and the entire architectural complex, as adapted, became the setting before which Pope Alexander III met with the German king Frederick Barbarossa (1177).

The great Florentine sculptor and architect Jacopo Sansovino (1486–1570) redesigned the piazza, linking it to the piazzetta. He is also responsible for the **Library**. Towards the close of the 16C, attention was turned to the redevelopment of the south side of the piazza and old buildings were removed to make way for the **Procuratie Nuove**.

The present trachyte paving was designed by Andrea Tirali (c.1657–1737), who also resurfaced the area known as the **Piazzetta dei Leoncini** named after the two lions by Giovanni Bonazza (1654–1736). Tirali then conceived the idea of accenting lines of perspective in the piazza by inlaying four "fasciae" in Carrara marble in concentric geometrical formation. Two such bands converge on the Basilica; the other two running oblique to the first pair align with the columns of St Mark and St Theodore. At their

Piazza San Marco and Basilica di San Marco

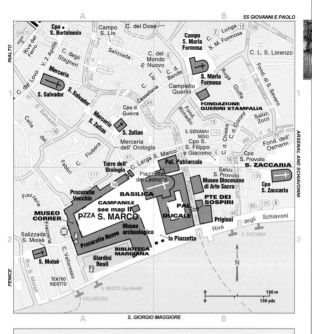

SS GIOVANNI E PAOLO

SAN MARCO

Seeing Piazza San Marco

Vaporetto: S. Marco. The square is the heart of the city. All central streets lead here. Two Venice must-see sights are here, the Basilica di San Marco, with its landmark campanile, and the Palazzo Ducale (Doges' Palace). Don't miss the piazza when an **orchestra** is playing outdoors near Caffè Florian or across at Quadri: a thoroughly romantic, magical experience. For a tour of the basilica, the Doges' Palace and the museums, allow at least a half day. Prepare to be immobilised by crowds in summer and on special occasions such as the Carnival. Early morning, evening and the small hours, and spring and autumn, when the colours and the sounds are crisp and clear, are infinitely preferable. **Kids** will love the view from the campanile, chasing pigeons, boarding a gondola, or a secret passages tour of the Doges' Palace.

PIAZZA SAN MARCO

speculative point of intersection stands the square base of the campanile (this is best appreciated from above).

This was little changed until its spectacular collapse on 14 July 1902. Miraculously, the only damage incurred was to Sansovino's Loggetta and to a small part of the Biblioteca Marciana. By 1911, the new campanile, an exact reproduction of the old one, had restored the square's traditional appearance.

The vast trapezoidal space (176m/577ft in length, 82m/269ft maximum width) is enclosed on the north side by the **Procuratie Vecchie** and by the later 16C Procuratie Nuove opposite.

In between, the Neoclassical Napoleon Wing or **Ala nuovissimo** was built in accordance with the wishes of Emperor Bonaparte after the demolition in the early 1800s of the 16C Sansovino Church of San Geminiano.

Basilica di San Marco★★★

(Saint Mark's Basilica) Open year-round Mon–Sat 9.45am–5pm (Nov–Easter Pala d'Oro and Treasury close 4pm), Sun and hols 2–5pm (Nov–Easter 4pm). Basilica free. Pala d'Oro €2. Treasury €3. Clothes must be appropriate for a place of worship; no large bags (leave these in the Ateneo San Basso (Piazzetta dei Leoncini); no photography or video cameras. 041 27 08 31. www.basilicasanmarco.it.

"Peace unto you, Mark, my Evangelist. Here rests your body," the angel said to St Mark near the Rialto, as the Evangelist was journeying from Aquileia to Rome.

Almost another 800 years were to elapse before the legendary prophecy was fulfilled: the symbol of St Mark has been synonymous with the Venetian flag ever since.

According to legend – In Egypt, around the year 800, two merchants set out for Alexandria with the intention of stealing the saint's remains whose relics would bestow upon Venice the prestige needed to "compete" with Rome or, at least, would affirm its politico-religious independence from the capital. The remains were taken in a chest aboard a Venetian vessel. On arrival in Venice, the precious relic was placed in the chapel of a castle belonging to Doge Giustiniano Partecipazio, and subsequently consecrated in 832 as the first church dedicated to St Mark.

History of the church – As a result of the arrival of the relics of San Marco, the first patron saint of Venice, San Teodoro (*Todaro* in dialect), was demoted, if not forgotten. After the fire of 976, which seriously damaged the church, St Mark's relics were lost. But, on the occasion of the consecration of the third church to be erected on this site (25 June 1094), a part of a pilaster in the right transept crumbled to reveal a human arm. The sacred relic was removed to the crypt and later buried below the high altar.

The 11C basilica, modelled upon the Church of the Holy Apostles in Constantinople, shows strong Eastern influence. The basilica became the pride of the Venetians and **Doge Domenico Selvo** (1071–84) would ask merchants travelling to the East to bring back marble and other prized stone (alabaster, jasper, porphyry, serpentine) for its

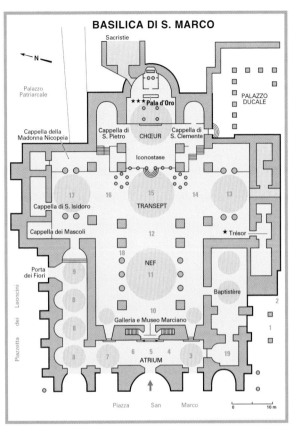

BASILICA DI S. MARCO

Sacristie

← N →

Palazzo Patriarcale

Palazzo Ducale

★★★ **Pala d'Oro**

Cappella della Madonna Nicopeia

Cappella di S. Pietro

CHŒUR

Cappella di S. Clemente

Iconostase

17 | 16 | 15 | 14 | 13

Cappella di S. Isidoro

TRANSEPT

Cappella dei Mascoli

12

★ Trésor

18

Porta dei Fiori

9

NEF
11

Baptistère

8

10

2

Galleria e Museo Marciano

8

1

8 | 7 | 6 | 5 | 4 | 3

19

ATRIUM

Leoncini

dei

Piazzetta

↑

Piazza   San   Marco

0   10 m

embellishment. So too began the mosaics in the domes and the vaults. **Exterior** – The basilica dominates Piazza San Marco, its portals, arches and five round 13C Byzantine domes remaining one of the most enduring images of Venice, silhouetted against the sky. Walk down the left flank of the basilica, overlooking Piazzetta dei Leoncini, to admire the Porta dei Fiori (4th arch, on the corner) with its Romanesque relief of *The Nativity*. The south side abuts the Doges'

Palace on the piazzetta. The first arch is framed by two columns surmounted with Romanesque griffins; the second arch contains the door to the Baptistery, framed with the **Acrean pillars** (1). Syrian in origin, two of the 6C columns are white marble, while the porphyry column, **pietra del bando**, is the proclamation stone from where laws would be announced. On the corner near the Palace stand the famous 4C **Tetrarchs★** (2) or Moors, thought to allude to the

29

Emperors Diocletian, Maximilian, Valerian and Constantine. Others claim they are Saracens who were turned to stone when trying to steal the treasure of St Mark.

Atrium

Guided tours (1hr) with biblical interpretations of the mosaics, Apr–Oct Mon–Sat 11am. No tours on holidays. Free. Arriving beneath the the Arch of Noah (4), the Arch of Paradise (5) and the Tower of Babel (6), start with the right dome, and follow towards the left.

Enter the basilica through the large atrium reserved for the unbaptised and new converts. Decked with mosaics that relate stories from the Old Testament, these herald others inside the church that illustrate episodes from the New Testament. At the end of the Fourth Crusade (1201–04), Venice gloried in its victory after the conquest of Constantinople. Romanesque and early Christian iconography in these early mosaics is borrowed from 5C–6C illuminated manuscripts that may have reached Venice with the Fourth Crusade.

Near the entrance are some of the oldest mosaics in the atrium, **The Creation according to Genesis** (3). Other mosaics here include the **Story of Abraham** (7) and **Story of Joseph** (8), concluding the Old Testament cycle with the **Story of Moses** (9). From there, a steep flight of stairs leads to the Galleria and the Museo di San Marco.

Museo di San Marco

Open year-round daily 9.45am–4.45pm. €5. 041 27 08 311. www.museosanmarco.it.

The Marciano Museum (access from the Gallery) offers a marvellous view of the mosaics and panorama of the piazza from the balcony. The collection of tapestries, mosaics and ancient basilica documents adds to the main draw, the **gilded bronze horses★★**.

Booty from the Fourth Crusade, they are probably either 4C–3C BC Greek or 4C Roman works. Given pride of place on the balcony, these wonderful equestrian statues were taken to Paris by Napoleon after his crushing Italian campaign, but returned in 1815 thanks in part

Interior, Basilica di San Marco

©Peter Barritt/age fotostock

MUST SEE

to skilled diplomatic negotiations by the artist Canova. In 1974 they were removed and restored; they were replaced with copies.

Mosaics★★★

Visitors are advised to view the mosaics inside St Mark's when the basilica is illuminated: Mon–Fri, 11.30am–12.30pm; Sat–Sun and holidays, all day.

Each mosaic offers something different, from Byzantine art to scenes by artists like Tintoretto and Veronese. The lower part of the walls depicts the saints, the middle section is reserved for the Apostles and the domes are dedicated to the Creator. The key to each story is in the dome of the apse from where the story unfolds chronologically. Note the Arch of the Apocalypse (10), West Arch (12), Dome of St Leonard (13), South Arch (14), Dome of the Ascension (15), North Arch (16) and Dome of St John the Evangelist (17).

Pala d'Oro★★★

The high altar holds the remains of St Mark. Beyond towers the great altarpiece. Commissioned and made in Constantinople in the 10C, the Golden Altarpiece is a masterpiece of the goldsmith's craft. Gleaming with precious stones set among enamelled panels, it continued to be embellished until the 14C.
The **Golden Altarpiece** is preceded by a ciborium on **columns of alabaster★★** inscribed with reliefs inspired by the Gospels and the Apocrypha. Their exact date and provenance remain uncertain, but may be 5C–6C Greek (from Ravenna), Syrian, Egyptian or Coptic.

Chapels

The **Pulpit of the Reliquary** was where the relics would be displayed and where the newly elected doge made his first appearance. Both chapels dedicated to **St Clement** (*right apse*) and **St Peter** (*left apse*) are screened off by their own iconostasis. Outside each chapel, wall mosaics (12C) illustrate episodes from the lives of St Mark and St Peter. The right window in the Chapel of St Clement enabled the doge to watch functions and services without leaving the comfort of his palace apartments. In the **Chapel of the Madonna Nicopeia** is a particularly venerated image of the Madonna and Child, called *Nicopeia* (Bringer of Victory or Leader), which served as the standard of the Byzantine army. Coming from Constantinople, the figure may have been booty from the Fourth Crusade.

Treasury★

This priceless collection of religious objects, reliquaries and ornaments came into Venice after the conquest of Constantinople in 1204.
Worthy of note is the *Artophoron*, an 11C container for the Bread of the Eucharist, in the shape of a church, crowned with oriental-style domes.

Baptistery

Open for prayer only.

The baptistery is divided into three interconnecting areas; 14C mosaics recount the life of John the Baptist and the Infant Jesus. The most famous panel shows *Salome Dancing before Herod.* The baptismal font is by Sansovino (1486–1570), who is buried here, before the altar.

🔺 Il Campanile★★

Open Jul–Sept 9am–9pm; April/
Easter–Jun and Oct 9am–7pm; rest
of year 9.30am–3.45pm. €8. 041 27
08 311. www.basilicasanmarco.it.

The Campanile has long served as
Venice's beacon – for ships as well
as tourists. Attractive yet perhaps
structurally unsound, the tower
has been rebuilt several times
over the centuries, achieving its
current look in the 16C. In 1902
it was completely destroyed and
had to be rebuilt from scratch to
the original design. The present
tower stands 96m/315ft high,
culminating in a golden angel
weathervane that turns in the wind.
Gigantic pilasters rise up to white
marble arches pierced by a four-
light loggia where the bells hang.
At the top, a magnificent **view**★★
stretches from the Giudecca Canal
to the Grand Canal across roofs and
chimneypots to the islands in
the lagoon.

Loggetta Sansoviniana
At the base of the tower, and facing
St Mark's, the richly decorated
Sansovino Loggetta comprises
three arches supported on columns
much like a triumphal arch;
columns also frame the niches
that accommodate the figures
of Minerva, Apollo, Mercury and
Peace. The reliefs above depict
(*from left to right*) the Island of
Candia, Venice as an allegory of
Justice, and the island of Cyprus.
The terrace at the front is enclosed
by a balustrade, broken in the
middle by a bronze gate designed
by Antonio Gai (1686–1769).
The present *loggetta* was first built
in the early 16C by **Jacopo Tatti
Sansovino**.

Palazzo Ducale★★★

(Doges' Palace). Open year-
round daily 9am–7pm (5pm
Nov–Easter). €12 Museums of
St Mark's Square ticket, also gives
entry to the Clock Tower, Museo
Correr, Museo Archeologico
Nazionale, Monumental Rooms of
Biblioteca Marciana plus one other
Musei Civici Veneziani (of your
choice). Itinerari Segreti (Secret
itinerary) tickets book online
(extra charge). 041 27 15 911.
www.museicivicivenezianivi.it.

The Doges' Palace almost dates
back to the origins of Venice itself.
For centuries an intricate power
system of checks and balances was
operated behind these walls. In
810 **Doge Agnello Partecipazio**
decided to locate the seat of his
public offices on the site of the
present Doges' Palace.
The buildings, which included the
Church of St Mark, were more of a
citadel than a government office.
The fortified residence gradually
gave way to offices to conduct
affairs of State and the building
evolved into the current Byzantine,
Gothic and Renaissance palace.
White and terracotta bricks, dark
arches and allegories of moral
example adorn the exterior.
Public announcements of capital
sentences were once announced
between the piazzetta's two red
marble columns; the executions
were held between the columns
of St Mark and St Theodore in
the square below.
The **Porta della Carta**★★, or "Paper
Doorway", is the palace's entrance.
The **Bridge of Sighs**★★ (**Ponte dei
Sospiri**) takes its name from the
plight of prisoners who were led
across it to the courtroom to learn

their fate, while catching glimpses of the enchanting view from the enclosed bridge's windows.

The bridge links the palace with the Prigioni Nuove (New Prisons). Inside, the bridge is divided into two passages through which visitors pass as they tour the Doges' Palace.

Inside the palace the magnificent statues of Mars and Neptune soon greet you, dominating the **Giant's Staircase**, at the top of which each new doge was crowned. From here, the **Golden Staircase** is an impressive sight, leading to the **Ducal Appartment**.

Ambassadors awaited their audience with the doge in the **Sala delle Quattro Porte** (Chamber of the Four Doors), while diplomatic delegations were housed in the **Sala dell'Anticollegio** antechamber. The doge's throneroom was the **Sala del Collegio** (college chamber), where he presided over meetings.

The "Full College" was occupied with and presented legal matters to the Senate, and with political relationships between Venice and diplomatic missions. In the **Sala del Senato**, the Senate Chamber,

or "Pregadi Chamber", members of the Senate were asked (*pregati*) to submit written requests to participate in the meetings. The assembly presided here over all matters of State.

The powerful and notorious Council of Ten, whose origins go back to 1310, convened in the **Sala del Consiglio dei Dieci**. The **Sala della Bussola** (Ballot Chamber) served as the waiting room for those to be interrogated by the heads (*capi*) of the Council of Ten. Next, the **Armeria** (Armoury rooms) house trophies, relics of war, the suit of armour of the infamous *condottiere* Gattamelata, and instruments of torture.

The enormous **Sala del Maggior Consiglio** (Grand Council Chamber) is perhaps the highlight of the tour. Here, and in the nearby Sala dello Scrutinio, the new doge was elected. The 76 doges who governed Venice from 804 to 1554, almost all painted by Domenico Tintoretto, are below the ceiling. Veronese's *Apotheosis of Venice* (1582) dominates the ceiling, while other paintings celebrate Venice's victory in battle. The long wall overlooking the Basin depicts

Sala del Maggior Consiglio, Palazzo Ducale

©Fondazione Musei Civici di Venezia

Courtyard, Palazzo Ducale

©Fondazione Musei Civici di Venezia

the Fourth Crusade. Behind the throne, *Paradiso*, the world's largest oil painting, was painted by Tintoretto, his son and followers. Votes were counted in the **Sala dello Scrutinio**. Portraits of the last 39 doges, 1556–1797, may be found here, including that of the last doge, **Ludovico Manin** (1789–97), who ceded to Napoleon, marking the subjugation of the Serenissima. The decoration of this room celebrates grandiose events in Venice's history.

The ceiling's most noteworthy paintings are *The Naval Victory of the Venetians over the Pisans at Rodi* by Vicentino and *The Venetian Victory over the Genoese at Trapani* by Giovanni Bellini.

Step up to the **Bridge of Sighs** (Prigioni Nuove) and across the canal to the New Prisons, which also served as the seat of the magistrature of the **Signori di Notte al Criminal**, a sort of vice squad. Note the graffiti scribbled on the stone walls.

The following rooms housed a judiciary body and magistrature, whose members, the *avogadori*, were lawyers appointed by the State. The palace corridors (*guided tours daily; reservations strongly encouraged; €17; book online; www.museicivicivenezian. it*) are a maze of hidden stairs and passageways that still exudes an air of mystery. The prison cells in the Palace were called the **Pozzi e Piombi** (Wells and Leads): the *pozzi* were the deep, damp dungeons for hardened criminals; the *piombi*, roofed in lead, were for those imprisoned for a couple of months. Life in the cells was not necessarily that severe: prisoners were allowed to bring some furniture and a little money with them.

Punishment was intended to induce remorse by exerting psychological pressure rather than by inflicting physical suffering. It was from the *piombi* that **Giacomo Casanova** (1725–98) made his daring escape, emerging onto the roof above the Grand Council Chamber.

The Procuratie
Procuratie Nuove

This was the seat of the Procurator, second only to the Doge. Planned by Scamozzi and completed by Longhena in the 17C under Napoleon, the Procuratie Nuove became the **Palazzo Reale**.

Museo Correr★★

To reach Museo Correr, go through the Ala Napoleonica. Same admission times, charges and contact details as Palazzo Ducale.
Teodoro Correr (1750–1830), a Venetian gentleman, bequeathed his rich history and art collection of the Serenissima to the city. Take the magnificent 19C staircase, through the Neoclassical **Sale Canoviane** (Canova Rooms) and on to the **History**, **Arts**, **Crafts** and **Games** Departments (*first floor*) where you will find some De' Barbari maps, Antonionio Canova sculptures and artefacts from city history.
The **Libreria dei Teatini** conserves books from the Teatini Convent, while the **Sale dei Costumi** feature official 17C and 18C garments worn by senators and procurators. Coinage is on display in the **Collezione Numismatica**, while the **Bucintoro** room displays the doge's unwieldy ship. On the second floor is the **Quadreria**

and its Venetian School paintings, as well as rooms devoted to the International Gothic style. Further rooms reveal works by Vivarini, Brueghel the Younger, Antonello da Messina, and the Bellinis, Jacopo, Giovanni, Carpaccio and Lorenzo Lotto.

Museo del Risorgimento

Housed on the same floor, this museum documents Venice after its 1797 surrender. Themes range from freemasonry to the rule of Napoleon and the Austrians. Return to Museo Correr's first floor to see Renaissance bronzes and a section on **Arts and Crafts** (*Arti e Mestieri*). The **Giochi** (Games) collection exhibits human pyramids that were "built" on wooden platforms on the Thursday before Lent, and bull-baiting.

Procuratie Vecchie

The original 12C residence of the Procurators, rebuilt after a 1512 fire. Take a break in Museo Correr's corridor café, with a few tables that have a lovely view of Piazza San Marco.

View of the grand staircase, Museo Correr

©Fondazione Musei Civici di Venezia

PIAZZA SAN MARCO

La Piazzetta

This extension of St Mark's Square, between the Doges' Palace and the Biblioteca Nazionale Marciana, overlooks St Mark's Basin where the canals converge. The two **Colonne di Marco e Todaro** frame the scene, supporting St Mark and St Theodore, brought back from the East in 1172. The latter is a copy: the original stands in the courtyard in the Doges' Palace. The lion, identified with St Mark, could be a chimera.

Biblioteca Nazionale Marciana★

Same admission times, charges and contact details as Palazzo Ducale.
As the first example of Classical architecture in Venice, this prestigious seat of Venetian culture is almost as glorious as its neighbour, the Doges' Palace. **Sansovino** worked on the library from 1537, although it was completed by Scamozzi. The Biblioteca's sculptural decoration draws on Classical mythology: leonine and mythological heads and statues overlook the piazzetta. **Jacopo De'Barbari**'s famous map of Venice is to be found here, as is the **Vestibule**, which became the Republic's Sculpture Museum when the Patriarch of Aquileia, Giovanni Grimani, donated his collection of sculpture and statuary to Venice. At the heart of the original Library, the **Sansovino Room** houses the codices and manuscripts bequeathed to the Republic by **Cardinale Bessarione** (1403–72), the famous Greek Humanist. The room's gruesome decoration is embellished with Mannerist paintings.

Museo Archeologico

Open year-round daily 8.15am–7.15pm (5pm Nov–Mar); last admission 30min before closing. Closed 1 Jan, 25 Dec. €4. 041 52 25 978. www.museiciviciveneziani.it.
World-class but under-visited, the Archaeological Museum is housed in the **Procuratie Nuove**, two doors away from the Biblioteca Marciana. Renaissance artists used these same Greek, Egyptian and Roman sculptures and fragments in their paintings. Among the ancient Archaic pieces are the famous **Grimani** Greek statues (5C–4C BC), as well as Assyrian-Babylonian, Egyptian, Cypriot, Mycenaen, early Venetian and Etruscan antiquities.

Torre dell'Orologio

Visit by guided tours only (must be booked in advance). In English, Mon–Wed 10am, 11am, 1pm; Thu–Sun 2pm, 3pm, 5pm. €12 Museums of St Mark's Square ticket (Palazzo Ducale) 041 52 09 070, or book online at www.museiciviciveneziani.it.
Designed by Codussi, the clock tower was erected between 1496 and 1499, and constitutes the main entrance to the **Mercerie**, Venice's principal shopping street (*see Rialto*). Atop, two Moors sound the hour on a big bell. Below stands the St Mark lion set against a starry background. A tour of the Renaissance Tower enables visitors to get a close view of the clock mechanism (cover your ears if you are there on the hour!); it ends on terraces which afford a magnificent view of St. Mark's Square and the whole city.

RIALTO★★

The first bridge (c.1175) to span the Grand Canal is situated in the heart of the commercial area. The Rialto Bridge links the long line of shops that snake from St Mark's Square to the Mercerie, as far as the side stalls and market in the San Polo district, passing a lively fish market on the way. Given the overwhelming hustle and bustle of the small workshops and local bars, it is easy to forget the long history of the Rialto, and the fact that it was once the seat of government in Venice.

Ponte di Rialto★★

The first Rialto bridge boosted commercial development of the area. The wooden bridge was replaced several times following its destruction during the uprisings led by Baiamonte Tiepolo, and twice more when it collapsed. Its design was further complicated by the requirements of the boatmen and the shopkeepers already established here. Palladio proposed a cumbersome Roman-style design with three arches, but this was dismissed on the grounds that it might hinder canal traffic. Some 80 years later, this consideration became less of an issue as restrictions were imposed upon larger ships using the Grand Canal. The new construction, designed by aptly named **Antonio da Ponte** (1512–97), was simplified to a single span, thereby ensuring ease of use by boats and barges as well as safeguarding a flow of water that prevented stagnation and maintained the delicate equilibrium of the lagoon.

The present bridge consists of a single stone archway, 28m/92ft long and 7.5m/25ft high, which supports a central alley lined with shop stalls, flanked on either side by a narrower parallel passageway. Access from one aisle of shops to another is from either end of the bridge or via transverse arches in the middle. The whole complex is sheltered by a sloping roof.

The Rialto remained the only bridge to span the Grand Canal until the mid-19C, when the Accademia Bridge and the Scalzi Bridge were built, and in 2008 the fourth bridge Ponte della Costituzione, nicknamed 'Calatrava' for its architect, was erected.

Ponte di Rialto

© Hoffmann Photography/age fotostock

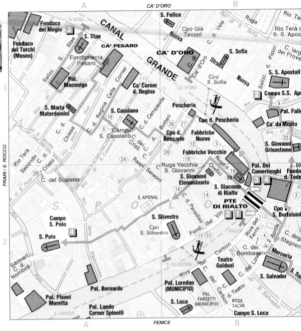

CA' D'ORO

CANAL GRANDE

FRARI / S. ROCCO

FENICE

A   B

Rialto Bridge and the Mercerie

🏛 Mercerie★

The large number of shops selling a variety of goods gives rise to the name of this historic commercial street. The *mercerie* (traditionally haberdashers selling cloth, ribbons and other merchandise, but now a catch-all term) provide access between St Mark's and the Rialto. This was the route chosen by nobles intending to make a triumphal entry into the Piazza San Marco. The Mercerie are as busy today as they were in the Middle Ages, and fall into three main sections, starting from the clock tower: Merceria dell'Orologio, Merceria di San Zulian and Merceria di San Salvador.

Campo San Bartolomeo

This *campo* is a busy crossroads between St Mark's, the Rialto, the Accademia and the Strada Nuova. Bars and tourist shops surround the square, which is dominated by a spirited late-19C **statue of Goldoni**.

San Zulian

Founded in the 9C but now cramped by adjacent buildings, the façade is nonetheless richly ornamented.

Above the portal, Tommaso Rangone, the benefactor of the church, is portrayed by Sansovino. Note also the columns that frame the cartouches and the windows below the pediments. Under the main tympanum is a typically Venetian feature, a *serliana*

MUST SEE

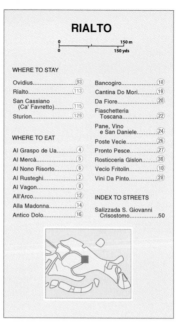

consisting of a window with three
openings, named after **Sebastiano
Serlio**. The church was remodelled
during the late Renaissance by
Sansovino and Alessandro Vittoria.
Of special interest are paintings by
Palma il Giovane and Veronese.

San Salvador

The 7C Church of San Salvador was
consecrated by Pope Alexander III
during his visit to Venice to meet
Barbarossa in 1177. The 17C
façade survives with a cannon ball
embedded in the masonry since
1849. The main layout by Spavento
combines Classical structural
elements with refined sculptural
ornament, a style that foreshadows
Mannerism and the bold Classicism
of Palladio.

Seeing the Rialto

Vaporetto: Rialto, San Marco.
Signposts all over the city centre
point visitors towards the Rialto.
In summer, spring and early
autumn, there is a near-continual
procession of tourists making
their way between the Rialto and
St Mark's Square. Allow about
4–5hrs for the listed routes, more
if you wish to shop along the
Mercerie.

Significant paintings include the
main altarpiece, *The Transfiguration*
by Titian (c.1490–1576) and, on
the right before the transept, his
Annunciation, as well as works by
Paris Bordone, Giovanni Bellini and
Francesco Vecellio.

RIALTO

39

Towards 🚶 Strada Nuova

This busy but attractive urban route between the Accademia and the Mercerie is thronged with shops.

Fondaco dei Tedeschi

This former association of German traders – the most powerful trading group in the city from the 13C onwards – now houses the main post office. Destroyed in a 1505 fire, the Fondaco (warehouse) was rebuilt by Giorgio Spavento and Scarpagnino. The frescoes that adorn the Grand Canal façade are the work of Giorgione and include the earliest known works by Titian. The two artists received the commission in part because they helped firefighters to put out the flames. More of the frescoes, subsequently removed, can be seen in the Ca' d'Oro (see Ca' d'Oro).

San Giovanni Crisostomo

In a narrow passageway is the red façade of the **Church of St John Chrysostom**, founded in 1080.

Campo Santi Apostoli

Strada Nuova begins at this square, a busy thoroughfare with shops and bars in the nearby calli. Note the **Church of All Saints** (dei Santi Apostoli) and its tall detached campanile. On the far side of the canal stands the 13C **Palazzo Falier**, named after its most eminent resident, **Doge Marino Falier**.

Beyond the Rialto Bridge

San Giacomo di Rialto

San Giacomo di Rialto is considered to be the oldest church in Venice. A document (of dubious origins) states that the city was born on 25 March 421 when three consuls arrived from Padua to establish a commercial seat at the Rialto. This church, partially hidden by the stalls and market in Campo San Giacomo di Rialto, celebrated that event. Venice's first public bank, **Banco Giro** (now a restaurant) was founded in 1619, just off the square.

Fabbriche Vecchie and Nuove

Now the Venice court, Scarpagnino designed the Fabbriche Vecchie and much of the surrounding area, later destroyed by fire in 1514. Sansovino designed the premises of the Fabbriche Nuove.

San Giovanni Elemosinario

Open Mon–Sat 10am–5pm. Closed 1 Jan, Easter, 15 Aug, 25 Dec. €3. 041 27 50 462. www.chorusvenezia.org. This ancient church was first built in 1071. Inside, there are works by Jacopo Palma il Giovane, Il Pordenone and Titian.

🚶 Campo della Pescheria

The Rialto's famous daily fish market bustles under the porticoes of an impressive modern (1907) building (closed Sundays and holidays). The vivacious **Campo delle Beccarie**, which once housed the public abattoir, now shelters a traditional Venetian bacaro (wine bar) and market stalls.

San Cassiano

San Cassiano dates back to the 9C. Its painting collection includes works by Bassano and Tintoretto.

Ca' Corner della Regina

After her fall from grace, here **Caterina Cornaro**, Queen of Cyprus, resided in her brother's Gothic palazzo. Modified in the

18C, Tiepolo-style frescoes recount the unhappy events of her life.

Santa Maria Mater Domini
This church near the 14C–15C Palazzo Zane has a distinctive five-arched window and a simple Istrian stone façade. Attributed to Sansovino, it might have been a project of **Pietro Lombardo** or **Codussi**. The interior is lavished with works by Tintoretto and Vicenzo Catena among others.

Ca' Pesaro★
Museums open Tue–Sun 10am–5/6pm; last admission 1hr before closing; €5.50 (combined 2 museums ticket with Ca d'Oro €6, 3 museums ticket with Ca d'Oro and Galleria Internazionale di Arte Moderna €11). 041 52 41 173. www.arteorientale.org. 041 72 11 27. www.museicivicivenezianianti.it.
Ca'Pesaro is home to important collections of oriental and modern art. The *palazzo*, commissioned by the Pesaro family, was begun by Longhena and completed by Antonio Gaspari. On the upper floor, the **Museo d'Arte Orientale** displays Japanese armour from the Edo Period (1615–1868), swords, lacquer-work, puppets, musical instruments and Chinese porcelain. The **Galleria Internazionale di Arte Moderna** features modern art from the end of the 19C onwards with work by the Futurists and other key movements.

Museo di Palazzo Mocenigo
Open year-round Tue–Sun 10am–5pm (Nov–Mar 4pm); last admission 30min before closing. Closed 1 Jan, 1 May, 25 Dec. €4. 041 72 17 98. www.museicivicivenezianianti.it.

Glimpse the life of the the Venetian nobility of the 17C and 18C. Palazzo Mocenigo was a Gothic palace modified as the 17C residence of the San Stae branch of the influential Mocenigo family. Seven became doges between 1414 and 1778; their portraits greet visitors in the entrance. See sumptuous fabrics and costumes from **Centro Studi di Storia del Tessuto e del Costume**, a foundation dedicated to their study and conservation.

Rialto to Campo S. Polo
Campo San Polo
This amphitheatre shaped *campo* is one of Venice's largest, making it a perfect venue for **events** – including open-air films during the Venice Film Festival – continuing its long tradition of ceremonies and entertainment.
Three notable *palazzi* face the square: the Gothic-style **Palazzo Soranzo**; the Baroque **Palazzo Tiepolo Maffetti**, with its distinctive head of Hercules (protector of commerce and merchants) over the portal; and, at the opposite corner, Sanmicheli's 16C **Palazzo Corner Mocenigo**, now the seat of the Guardia di Finanza (Finance Police).
The church of **San Polo** (*open Mon–Sat 10am–5pm; closed 1 Jan, Easter, 15 Aug, 25 Dec; €3; 041 27 50 462; www.chorusvenezia.org*) has stood here at least since the 9C. Inside, major works of art include the *Assumption of the Virgin*, and to its left a *Last Supper* by **Tintoretto**, as well as other pieces by Tiepolo, Giandomenico and Veronese.

LA FENICE ★

Situated between Piazza San Marco and the lower loop of the Grand Canal, this is a very lively part of Venice. Teatro La Fenice is one of Italy's top three venues for opera (the other two being La Scala and San Carlo). The area has elegant hotels and good shops: Campo San Luca for books; and for authentic papier mâché masks, look between Campo Manin and Campo Sant'Angelo. Around the Church of San Moisé are art, glass and bookbinding workshops.

San Moisé

If nothing succeeds like excess, **San Moisé** is probably the champion for Venetian church façades. This riot of sculptural ornamentation was built by Longhena's pupil Alessandro Tremignon in the 17C, assisted by Flemish artist Meyring, a disciple of Bernini. The façade bursts with garlands, festoons, sculpture and other ornamentation. The lower tier houses a triumphal arch memorializing the Fini family. The busy Baroque interior is home to Tintoretto's dramatic *Christ Washing his Disciples' Feet* (in the chapel).

Campo San Fantin

Campo San Fantin is a secluded and picturesque little square. The Renaissance church **Chiesa San Fantin** was begun by Scarpagnino (active in Venice 1505–1549) and completed by Sansovino. Inside are two works by Palma il Giovane (1544–1628). On the other side of the *campo* is the school for science, literature and art, **Ateneo Veneto** (*open Mon–Fri, 10am–1pm & 3–7pm, library 9.30am–5.30pm; closed holidays, Aug, 21 Nov, 23 Dec–6 Jan; 041 52 24 459, www.ateneoveneto.org*), formerly home to the **Scuola di San Fantin** or **Scuola di Santa Maria della Consolazione** (whose role was to console condemned prisoners on their way to execution) **and San Girolamo**, patron saint of scholars. The front (c.1580) was designed by Alessandro Vittoria. Since 1812 it has been the **Ateneo Veneto**. The Aula Magna on the ground floor has a fine wooden panelled ceiling decorated by Palma il Giovane; the Aula Tommaseo houses works by Antonio Zanchi (1631–1722)

Gran Teatro La Fenice

Vaporetto: S. Marco, S. Maria del Giglio, S. Samuele, S. Angelo or Rialto. The area in the immediate vicinity of the theatre is known as the "seven campi between the bridges," a reference to the Campi di San Bartolomeo, San Salvador, San Luca, Manin, Sant'Angelo, Santo Stefano and San Vidal, situated between the Rialto Bridge and Accademia Bridge. Although the theatre occupies a fairly quiet setting, it is edged by a bustling commercial hub of restaurants and shops. Don't miss the designer boutiques and street entertainers along the Calle Larga 22 Marzo. Allow 2hrs for the itinerary and another 1hr for a guided tour of the theatre.

(*ceiling and, on entering, the right wall*) and Francesco Fontebasso (1709–69) (*opposite*). The Sala di Lettura (Reading Room) is decorated by Veronese (1528–88).

🔍 Gran Teatro La Fenice★
Guided tours (45min) daily 10am–6pm unless theatre is being used for other purposes. Closed 1 Jan, 1 May, 25 Dec. €8. 041 78 65 11. www.teatrolafenice.it, www.festfenice.com.

This famous opera house and music-theatre was inaugurated in 1792 after its predecessor (1673) burned down in 1774. Construction was initiated by Giannantonio Selva (1751–1819), a friend of Canova, who won the commission in a competition. Almost completely destroyed by fire in 1836, it was rebuilt and renamed La Fenice (The Phoenix) in honour of its emergence from the ashes. Neoclassical in style, La Fenice had two façades and two entrances, including one overlooking the canal. The auditorium appears bigger than the façade, a problem overcome by means of an ingenious series of stairways. This "jewel box of a theatre" (Isaac Sterne) burned down again on 29 January 1996. Special funds were set up by the

Italian government, the Venice in Peril Fund and the American Save Venice Committee. Reconstructed to architect Aldo Rossi's plan, the theatre reopened in 2003.

Campo San Maurizio
This tranquil square becomes a busy three-day 🔍**antiques market** four times a year (see tourist board website). To the right of the church is a view of the campanile of Santo Stefano. The former **Scuola degli Albanesi**, with its Renaissance reliefs, sits on the left. Previous residents of the *palazzo* opposite include the novelist Alessandro Manzoni (1785–1873) and Giorgio Baffo (1694–1768), who wrote salacious poetry in Venetian dialect.

🔍 Campo Santo Stefano
One of the most elegant squares in the city, this *campo* is dominated by a church that also hosts concerts. It is a lively meeting place animated by busy outdoor cafés and people making their way to and from the Accademia Bridge, enjoying the evening *passeggiata*. Towering over the square is a monument (1882) to **Niccolò Tommaseo** (1802–74), journalist and essayist. **Palazzo Loredan** is

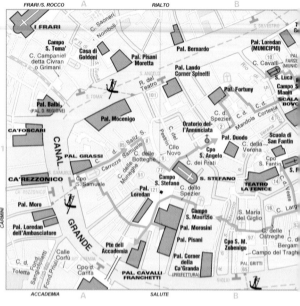

Map labels:
FRARI / S. ROCCO   A   RIALTO   B
I FRARI
C. Saoneri
Nomboli
S. SILVESTRO
Campo S. Toma'
Casa di Goldoni
C. Campaniel detta Civran o Grimani
Pal. Pisani Moretta
Pal. Bernardo
Pal. Loredan (MUNICIPIO)
Cavalli
FARSE (MUNIC)
R. del Teatro
Pal. Lando Corner Spinelli
S. Luca
Campo S. Manin
SCALA BOVO
Pal. Fortuny
S. TOMA
Pal. Balbi (PAL. D. REGIONE)
Pal. Mocenigo
C. d. Spezier
C. d. Mandola
Oratorio dell'Annunciata
CA'FOSCARI
Verona
Cortesia
Scuola di San Fantin
Pal. Duodo
CANAL
Saliz. S. Samuele
C. del Pestrin
C. della Verona
PAL. GRASSI
C. Cllo Novo
Cpo S. Angelo
Carrozze
C. delle Bottegha
C. dei Frati
Cpo S. Fantin
S. F
CA'REZZONICO
Cpo S. Samuele
C. delle Meneghe
Campo S. Stefano
S. STEFANO
TEATRO LA FENICE
Pal. Loredan
C. dello Spezier
Pal. Moro
Campo S. Maurizio
S. Maria del Giglio
C. Larg
Pal. Loredan dell'Ambasciatore
GRANDE
Pal. Morosini
C. delle Ostreghe
Pte dell'Accademia
Pal. Pisani
Cpo S. M Zobenigo
Bergam
Calle Corfu
Fond. Sangiantoffetti
Cpo d. Carita
Pal. Corner della Ca'Granda (PREFETTURA)
PAL GRITTI
Campo del Tragh
C. d. Toletta
Fond. Priuli
PAL. CAVALLI FRANCHETTI
GIGLIO
ACCADEMIA   A   SALUTE   B
CARMINI

home to the Venetian Institute of Science, Arts and Letters and its prestigious library (*open Mon–Fri 9am–12.45pm, 1.30–5pm; 041 24 07 711; www.istitutoveneto.it*). In 1536 the Loredan family commissioned Scarpagnino (active in Venice 1505–49) to rebuild the palace, which had recently been acquired from the Mocenigo family. Note its Palladian northern façade. **Palazzo Pisani**, one of the largest private palaces in the city, is on the square of the same name. Having been acquired by a noble family between the 17C and 18C, Girolamo Frigimelica (1653–1732) was commissioned to remodel the building. The palazzo is now the home of the Benedetto Marcello Music Conservatory.
Palazzo Morosini dates to the 14C and was restored at the end of the 17C by Antonio Gaspari.

Former residents include Francesco Morosini, Doge 1688–94. It is now home to the New Consortium of Venice, a group of 40 companies set up in 2005 with a remit to save the city from the encroaching sea.

Palazzo Grassi

Erected in 1749 by Giorgio Massari, this was the last Venetian palace to be built before the fall of the Republic. The outdoor steel sculpture, *Balloon Dog* (2000), is by Jeff Koons. Inside, the courtyard has a fine colonnade and a grand staircase frescoed with masked figures by Alessandro Longhi. Other rooms are frescoed by Jacopo Guarana (1720–1808) and Fabio Canal (1703–67). Open during temporary exhibitions (*041 52 31 680; www.palazzo grassi.it*), it has a good café and bookshop.

S. GIORGIO MAGGIORE

Santo Stefano★

*Mon–Sat 10am–5pm. Closed 1 Jan,
Easter, 15 Aug, 25 Dec. €3. 041 27
50 462. www.chorusvenezia.org.*

Construction of St Stephen's and
the adjacent convent was begun
in the latter half of the 13C; the
church was modified in the 15C.
The campanile (60m/196ft 10in
tall) is one of the most famous
in Venice. In 1585 it was hit by
lightning so violent that the bells
melted. Further damage was
incurred by subsidence during the
17C and 18C, which left the tower
leaning at an angle, as do many
bell towers in Venice. St Stephen's is
a pantheon to the glory of the city:
it contains the tombs of **Giovanni
Gabrieli** (composer and organist)
and of **Francesco Morosini** (doge
1688–94), as well as Baldassare
Longhena's monument to Captain
Bartolomeo d'Alviano. Tintoretto's
Last Supper has a dog and cat that
allude to the dispute between the
Catholic and Protestant Churches
over the mystery of the Eucharist.

Campo Sant'Angelo

Northeast of Campo Santo Stefano,
Campo Sant'Angelo is bordered
by some handsome *palazzi*
overlooking the canal.
The **Oratorio dell'Annunciata**
(Oratory of the Annunziata)
replaced the church that gave the
square its name, and the Scuola dei
Zoti, the guild for disabled sailors.
The plaque on **Palazzo Duodo**
commemorates the composer
Domenico Cimarosa (1749–1801),
who died here. The Gothic portal
on the bridge leads into the
cloisters of St Stephen (now the
headquarters of the Regional
Accountancy Board).

LA FENICE

Palazzo Fortuny

Dating to the 15C, the building boasts two mullioned windows with five arches. The Palazzo Pesaro degli Orfei was acquired by the painter, photographer, stage designer and textile designer, **Mariano Fortuny y Madrazo** (1871–1949), in 1899.

Formerly a music school, the palace now houses a museum, **Museo Fortuny** (*open Wed–Mon 10am–6pm; last admission 5pm; closed 1 Jan, 25 Dec; €4; 041 52 00 995, www.museicivicivenezziani.it*), which is devoted to the artist's work and houses temporary exhibits.

Campo Manin

You can get an idea of modern Venetian architecture from the shops down one side of Campo Manin and the **Cassa di Risparmio di Venezia**, designed by Pierluigi Nervi (1891–1979) and Angelo Scattolin. Note the monument to **Daniele Manin** (1875).

Scala del Bovolo

041 53 22 920. www.scalabovolo.org.

The delicate spiral **Bovolo Staircase** is near a tiny, peaceful courtyard. The staircase (*bovolo* in Venetian dialect) harmoniously blends Gothic and Renaissance styles. Encased in a tower, the staircase provides access to the palazzo's loggias, and at the top offers a lovely **view★★** over Venetian rooftops.

🚶 Campo San Luca

One of the most popular meeting places in Venice, this lively *campo* is lined with cafés, well-known stores, bookshops, travel agencies and fast-food outlets, and is close to many shops. The **Church of St Luke** (San Luca) has Veronese's (1528–88) *Virgin in Glory Appearing to St Luke While Writing the Gospel* by Calle Goldoni. On the opposite side of the *campo*, Calle del Teatro leads to **Teatro Goldoni**, named in honour of Italy's famed playwright, Carlo Goldoni. Venice once had many theatres; now those regularly active are La Fenice, the Goldoni and the Teatro Màlibran, although alternative spaces are used including churches, conservatories and museums. From here, you can walk back to Piazza San Marco via the **Bacino Orseolo**, likely to have several of the city's gleaming black gondolas at rest in a dock.

San Salvador

The 7C Church of San Salvador was consecrated by Pope Alexander III during his visit to Venice to meet Barbarossa in 1177. Its 17C façade has had a cannonball embedded in the masonry since 1849. The main layout was designed by Spavento, who foreshadows Mannerism and the bold Classicism of Palladio. Inside, three square bays are aligned to form a nave, each cubic space rising to a semicircular dome. A number of significant paintings include the main altarpiece, *The Transfiguration* by **Titian** (c.1490–1576), and, in the last bay, his *Annunciation*. To the right of the main chapel hangs *The Martyrdom of St Theodoric* by Paris Bordone (1500–71). In the Santissimo Chapel on the left of the main altar is *The Disciples at Emmaus* by **Giovanni Bellini** (c.1432–1516); the organ doors (*by the side door*) are painted by Titian's brother, Francesco Vecellio (1475–1560).

ACCADEMIA ★★★

The area around Venice's famous Academy of Fine Art is under permanent invasion: locals go about their everyday business, visitors arrive on the *vaporetti* in search of art treasures, and students mill around outside the nearby university, lending a bohemian atmosphere. Whatever your business here, it's always a good spot for a short break at one of the bars or trattorias.

Gallerie dell' Accademia ★★★

Open 8.15am–7.15pm (2pm Mon), last admission 45min before closing. The gallery limits the number of people allowed in at any one time, so if you are visiting at a busy time of year, book ahead either online or by telephone. Closed 1 Jan, 1 May, 25 Dec. €6.50. 041 52 00 345. www.gallerieaccademia.org.

The **Academy of Fine Art** exhibits the city's most important collection of Venetian art assembled to preserve its heritage and to instruct art students, showcasing the development of Venetian painting from the 14C to the 18C. Buildings converted to form the gallery include the **Monastery of Lateran Canons**, designed by Andrea Palladio (1508–80), the **Church of La Carità**, an atmospheric building that was redesigned by Bartolomeo Bon (recorded 1441–64), and the **Scuola Santa Maria della Carità**, the first Scuola Grande, which was erected in 1260. The tour starts in the large Sala Capitolare at the top of the 18C staircase. Be sure to seek out artists who may be unfamiliar, too, as many show remarkable bravura.

🎨 Interpreting the Art

Like many museums, the best way to approach the Accademia is to keep any eye out for the masterpieces, but to also use it as a way of discovering less familiar artists. Look for portraits and sumptuous Venetian interiors, portrayals of the pageantry of formal visits, seascapes and landscapes – all are full of revelations about daily life, social conventions, customs and traditions.

Detail, Apparition of the Crucified of Mount Ararat in the Church of Sant' Antonio di Castello, Carpaccio, c.1512, Gallerie dell' Accademia

© ripimages

ACCADEMIA

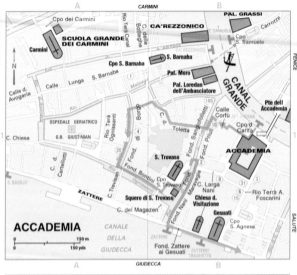

Venetians were renowned for their sumptuous colours, but that doesn't mean they neglected perspective, drama or lighting. Keep in mind that in many paintings – especially religious ones – nothing is there by chance, but each is charged with meaning, sometimes double or even conflicting, which may be lost to the modern viewer. Even illiterate Venetians of centuries past would have picked up these clues immediately – from their own religious instruction and folklore. If you have time, you will enjoy "decoding" these symbols. Some by now may be familiar, like the lion that symbolises St Mark – and also

Venice. Objects or figures that may seem like bit players on a stage require a greater leap of deduction and some historical background to understand; for example, that the dog and cat inserted in one larger scene symbolize feuding Catholic and Protestant factions. Whether or not you have the time or inclination for such detective work, one thing is guaranteed at the Accademia: the stunning beauty of the works themselves.

Highlights

The **Venetian Gothic** style set the way for what came later in the Renaissance. You will find works by better-known **Paolo**

Vaporetto: Accademia or Zattere. The Dorsoduro *sestiere* of Venice on the north side hosts the Gallerie dell'Accademia. The south side boasts the Zattere, the long promenade that overlooks the Giudecca Canal and Giudecca Island. Every imaginable type of boat floats by, including ocean liners that are outsize in scale for this canal. Don't miss the Accademia Gallery, of course, and the picturesque gondola dockyard, Squero di San Trovaso. New galleries and museum spaces have opened in recent years, too. Allow 2hrs for the Academy Gallery and 1hr for the area.

and **Lorenzo Veneziano**, but see also **Michele Giambino**, given credit for launching and refining this important movement in 14C Venice. The first room shows not only the bravura of the painters, but various stories their altarpieces were intended to emphasize. **Bellini** and **Carpaccio** show wonderful interplays of colour and work in drama. **Mantegna**, who influenced Bellini, was brilliant with his enigmatic images that convey a sense of mystery, wonder and sometimes curiosity. Look for savvy psychological interpretations, with characters that range from delicate, humble and fragile, to ruthless. **Lorenzo Lotto** conveys a sense of contemplation and distraction in a scholar, **Giorgione**'s old woman is well aware that her youthful allure has abandoned her. The story of each painting would make a fascinating tale, but some are particularly dramatic. Think of **Veronese**, who, when confronted by an Inquisition tribunal that took offence at the sumptuousness of his *Last Supper*, changed the name of the painting to *The Feast in the House of Levi*, a strategy that perhaps carried its own risks. **Bonifacio de' Pitati** may not be a familiar artist, but his painting offers a cross-section of Venetian culture, social classes and activities:

some have not changed much in modern times, like young lovers oblivious to their surroundings. Surprisingly few **Canaletto** scenes are here, as most wound up abroad, or at least elsewhere in Italy, but there are plenty of other Venetian landscapes to admire.

The **cityscapes** and **genre paintings** offer snapshots of the Venice that was and in some cases still is. Look for the Rialto when it was still wood, La Fenice before it burned (or burned again), bell towers and merchants hawking wares. Pore over the details of interiors and clothing and compare them with what you can see today throughout Venice or in the costume-maker's window.

In case you need to see one more masterpiece on your way out, the Accademia has thoughtfully hung **Titian**'s *Presentation of the Virgin at the Temple* (1530), a reminder of how important the collection is.

Zattere

If the crowds of the museum or neighbourhood don't enhance your artistic idyll, head for the **Zattere** for fresh air, an outdoor café, and some modes of transport that Renaissance artists never could have seen, as well as others that look exactly like what you've just viewed in the paintings.

ACCADEMIA

Church of Santa Maria del Rosario (Gesuati)

©Oleg Seleznev/Dreamstime.com

⚜️ Walking Tour

Ponte dell'Accademia

This famous landmark wooden bridge, one of only four bridges that cross the Grand Canal, links the *sestieri* of San Marco (near elegant Campo di San Stefano) with Dorsoduro (at the Accademia), then canals and walks lead to the Zattere with its busy seafaring canal. Pause on the bridge to take photos with the Grand Canal as a picturesque backdrop.

Rio Ognissanti

To reach the Zattere from the Accademia you can go via the Rio Terrà degli Ognissanti, a former canal landfilled in 1867. "Rio terà" in Venetian dialect means interrupted canal – ie part of a canal filled with earth to create a pedestrian route.

Chiesa San Trovaso

Entrance on the canal side.
Built in the 9C, architects of the Palladian School modified San Trovaso 16C–17C. Built in the plan of a Latin cross, this has paintings by Tintoretto, his son Domenico, Palma il Giovane and others.

Squero di San Trovaso

Gondolas are repaired, often in full view, in this *squero*, one of the few still in operation in Venice. This is the most famous, in part because its idiosyncratic wood building, brightened in summer with geraniums, looks like an alpine chalet. Artisans in this **boatyard** build and repair gondolas, to the delight of intrigued onlookers on the opposite side of the canal.

Gesuati

Mon–Sat 10am–5pm. Closed 1 Jan, Easter, 15 Aug, 25 Dec. €3. 041 27 50 462. www.chorusvenezia.org.
Santa Maria del Rosario ai Gesuati, a famous landmark church on the Zattere, faces the water. Remodelled in the late 17C, the façade is similar to San Giorgio Maggiore. Inside is a *Crucifixion* by Tintoretto, *Three Saints* by Piazzetta (1683–1754) and a *Madonna* by **Giambattista Tiepolo**.

Chiesa della Visitazione

This Church of the Visitation boasts two fine ceiling paintings by **Giambattista Tiepolo**.

LA SALUTE ★★

Despite the hordes of tourists visiting the landmark church of Santa Maria della Salute and the famous Guggenheim Collection of modern art, this corner of the Dorsoduro *sestiere* seems spacious and peaceful. Mostly residential, it has few shops, cafés and wine bars (most are in San Trovaso and San Barnaba districts). Foreign artists' workshops, the Anglican Church, and numerous American and British tourists give these streets an Anglo-American flavour.

 Walking Tour

Le Zattere ★

A walk along the *fondamente* with a perfect view over the wide Giudecca Canal offers a bustling, non-stop show of boats and vessels of all sizes and shapes, with the Island of Giudecca on the opposite side as backdrop. Relax in the open air at a pavement café or restaurant, even in winter if the sun's out and it's not too chilly. Logging operations, like those of Titian's family, would shoot their logs by river down from the Veneto tied in *zattere*, wooden rafts. The architecture harks back to days of hard physical work and profound religious faith: the former **Magazzini del Sale**, a 14C salt warehouse; the Convent and **Church of the Spirito Santo**, from where the bridge of boats stretches

across the water for the Feast of the Redentore; and the **Ospedale degli Incurabili** (Hospital for Incurables), which became an orphans' home, then music conservatory.

La Dogana

A 17C modification made the 15C Dogana da Mar, the customs entry point for goods arriving by sea, resemble a ship's hull. Since 2009 the François Pinault Foundation has run **Punto della Dogana** here, a contemporary art centre. Outside is the *Fortune* sculpture.

Santa Maria della Salute ★★

Open year-round daily 9am–noon and 3–6pm. 041 27 43 911. www.seminariovenezia.

The Basilica of Santa Maria della Salute is one of the most important sights on Venice's skyline. In 1630, when Venice was racked by

Santa Maria della Salute

©imagebroker/hemis.fr

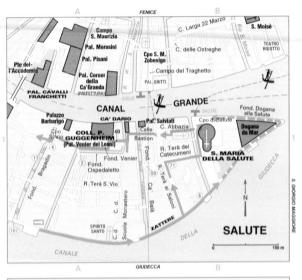

Map labels:
- FENICE
- A
- B
- Campo S. Maurizio
- Pal. Morosini
- Pal. Pisani
- Pte del-l'Accademia
- Pal. Corner della Ca'Granda (PREFETTURA)
- PAL. CAVALLI FRANCHETTI
- C. Larga 22 Marzo
- S. Moisè
- Cpo S. M. Zobenigo
- C. delle Ostreghe
- TEATRO RIDOTTO
- PAL GRITTI
- Campo del Traghetto
- CANAL
- GRANDE
- SALUTE
- Fond. Dogana alla Salute
- Palazzo Barbarigo
- CA' DARIO
- Pal. Salviati
- Cpo d. Salute
- Dogana da Mar
- Cpo S. Vio
- COLL. P. GUGGENHEIM (Pal. Venier dei Leoni)
- 40
- Calle Bastion
- C. Abbazia
- R. Terà dei Catecumeni
- S. MARIA DELLA SALUTE
- Fond. Venier
- Fond. Ospedaletto
- R. Terà S. Vio
- R. Terà al Saloni
- GIUDECCA
- SPIRITO SANTO
- Scuola Monastero
- ZATTERE
- DELLA
- SALUTE
- CANALE
- A
- GIUDECCA
- B
- N
- 0   150 m
- S. GIORGIO MAGGIORE

plague, the citizens pledged to erect a church should the epidemic subside.

Their prayers were answered, and in 1631 the prestigious architect **Baldassare Longhena** developed the project.

This impressive basilica has a magnificent flight of steps to the entrance. The great round dome emerges from an octagonal base: its eight façades hold a figure flanked by two angels over each pediment. Like Palladio, Longhena used Classical forms to form bold outlines.

Figurative sculpture relieves flat planes and reiterates the human dimension. Born into a family of stonecarvers, it's no surprise that

Longhena added a proliferation of statues. The church itself is akin to a free-standing sculpture, occupying a prominent position from every viewing angle.

At the apex, a Madonna clutches the baton of the *Capitano da Mar* (Captain-General of the Sea), poised above the lantern.

The patron presides over the façade's main pediment.

On the smaller dome stands St Mark, flanked by weathervanes of the two *campanili* that mark the far end of the church.

The drum, of great concentric volutes known as *orecchioni* (big ears), links the lower level of the outer section with the dome. The main cupola opens into six chapels,

MUST SEE

Vaporetto: Salute, Accademia. The Salute area faces the portion of the San Marco *sestiere* near the Gritti Palace. Edging the south side of the Grand Canal and extending eastward towards St Mark's Basin, the opposite bank extends to the Zattere, the long promenade along the Giudecca Canal. Sit near the broad steps of La Salute for a moment, to take in the sights and sounds of the Grand Canal, where an egret might alight to fish. The Zattere is wider and allows for ship traffic to pass that cannot navigate the Grand Canal, including even ocean liners, outsize leviathans that seem to exceed the scale not only of the canal, but of Venice itself. Allow about 3hrs for the walking tour, plus another hour for the Guggenheim Collection.

the polychrome marble floor converging on a central circle of five roses to suggest a rosary. The health (*salute*) and salvation accorded to Venice emanates from its legendary birth date on the Feast of the Annunciation (25 March 421), thus protected by the Virgin. Paintings to see include *Descent of the Holy Spirit,* painted by **Titian** (1490–1576) in 1555, and a 12C icon, the *Madonna della Salute*. The sculptural group above (1670–74) represents Venice, liberated from the plague, at the Virgin's feet, by Flemish artist Juste Le Court (1627–79). The plague is chased away by the angel.
In the sacristy don't miss the *Wedding at Cana* by **Tintoretto** (1518–94), who painted himself as the first Apostle on the left, as well as his friends and their wives. Images of the *Madonna in Prayer* are by **Sassoferrato**. In the corridor before the chapels are three altarpieces by **Luca Giordano**.

Collezione Peggy Guggenheim★★
Open year-round Wed–Mon 10am–6pm. Last admission 1hr before closing. Closed 25 Dec. €10. 041 24 05 411. www.guggenheim-venice.it.

The Peggy Guggenheim Collection is housed in the incomplete **Palazzo Venier dei Leoni** (1749), designed by Lorenzo Boschetti, architect of the Church of St Barnabas. The peaceful garden has two wall stones that mark the final resting places of the owner and her beloved dogs. Peggy was the niece of American industrialist, Solomon R Guggenheim, who founded his own museum designed by Frank Lloyd Wright in New York. Peggy began her Venice collection in 1938 and acquired the palazzo after the Second World War. She lived there until her death in 1979. According to her wishes, both the palazzo and the collection were handed over to the Solomon Guggenheim Foundation.
The gallery houses a superb collection of modern art and most major movements are represented, including examples from Picasso's Cubist period, though it is particularly strong in **Surrealist art**. It contains works by Braque, Picasso, Mondrian, Boccioni, Brancusi, Kandinsky, Chagall, Mirò, De Chirico, Ernst, Klee, Magritte, Dalí, Pollock, Calder, Vasarely and Moore. The Guggenheim also holds the **Mattioli Collection** and its 26 Futurist masterpieces.

SCHIAVONI & ARSENALE★

Aresenale's historic shipyard and landmark towers hint at Venice's former naval prowess. Venice flourished as a maritime power, in particular due to the quality of her ships. Behind the bustling Riva degli Schiavoni waterfront is a quiet and atmospheric part of Castello, the largest of Venice's *sestieri*, and a tranquil break from the dense crowds of St Mark's Square, just a few minutes' walk away. Schiavoni is a reference both to Slavs from Schiavonia (today's Dalmatia) and to slaves, a reminder of the darker historic aspects of the Republic.

🐾 Walking Tour

Rive degli Schiavoni

From the Doge's Palace, walk east along the 9C route that leads toward Giardini Pubblici and Arsenale. San Marco Basin is busy with boat traffic of all shapes and sizes (note *vaporetto* docks for your return trip or to head for other islands). Palazzi with historic hotels, cafés and restaurants are separated by narrow canals, where smaller vessels enter and exit as you pass above on the footbridges.

La Pietà

Santa Maria della Visitazione became known as "La Pietà" (the merciful one) for its hospice for abandoned children, dedicated in the 14C. In the 18C, the church was redesigned as a concert hall, since the orphans' education emphasised music, for a time under the leadership of **Antonio Vivaldi**. Inside, the building is vaulted to optimise acoustics. The orchestra and choir are positioned along the side walls, while frescoes with musical themes adorn the ceiling.

🚢 Museo Storico Navale★

Open Mon–Sat 8.45am–1.30pm (1pm Sat). Closed holidays. €1.55. 041 24 41 399 or 041 52 00 276. www.marina.difesa.it.

Design and boat enthusiasts will delight in this treasure trove of Venice's shipbuilding industry. Artefacts range from scale models of the city and her fortresses to Peggy Guggenheim's gondola. The **ground floor** displays weaponry

Arsenale

MUST SEE

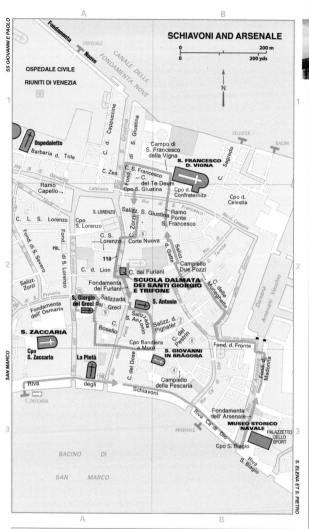

SCHIAVONI AND ARSENALE

0   200 m
0   200 yds

N

OSPEDALE CIVILE
RIUNITI DI VENEZIA

Fondamenta Nuove

CANALE DELLE FONDAMENTA NOVE

Ospedaletto
Barbaria d. Tole

C. Cappuccine

S. Giustina

CELESTIA

BACINI

Campo di S. Francesco della Vigna

S. FRANCESCO D. VIGNA

C. S. Francesco
C. del Te Deum
Cpo S. Giustina
Cpo d. Confraternita

Cpo d. Celestia

C. Zen
Fond. S. di

Ramo Capello

Salizz. S. Giustina

Ramo Ponte S. Francesco

S. LORENZO

Cpo S. Lorenzo

C. S. Lorenzo

C. d. Lion

118

C. dei Furlani

SCUOLA DALMATA DEI SANTI GIORGIO E TRIFONE

Campiello Due Pozzi

C. delle Mungnette

Arsenale Vecchio

Darsena

Corte Nuova

Fondamenta dei Furlani

S. Giorgio dei Greci

Salizzada dei Greci

S. Antonin

C. Bosello

Cpo Bandiera e Moro

Salizz. d. Pignater

C. del Pestrin

Fond. d. Fronte

S. ZACCARIA

Cpo S. Zaccaria

La Pietà

degli

C. dei Dose

S. GIOVANNI IN BRAGORA

Campiello della Pescaria

Riva

Schiavoni

Fondamenta dell' Arsenale

MUSEO STORICO NAVALE

PALAZZETTO DELLO SPORT

Cpo S. Biagio

Riva S. Biagio

ARSENALE

BACINO DI SAN MARCO

SAN MARCO

S. ELENA ET S. PIETRO

WHERE TO STAY

Liassidi Palace.................. 75

STREET INDEX

S. Giorgio degli Schiavoni
(Fondamenta)..............118

WHERE TO EAT

Ai Corazzieri.....................② 2
Al Covo............................④ 4
Alle Alpi da Dante............⑥ 6
Corte Sconta....................⑧ 8
Da Remigio.......................⑨ 9
MET..................................⑩ 10

Vaporetto: S. Zaccaria, Arsenale or Riva degli Schiavoni. East of Piazza San Marco, Castello is home to the relatively quiet and secluded Arsenale district, which still bears the imprint of artisans and workers that toiled in the complex and immense world of shipbuilding. Schiavoni frames the Castello district on the south, bisected by the wide Rio di San Agostini. Here you will see laundry flapping across streets and canals, an ocean liner passing so close it seems ready to dock on the pavement, and evidence of Venice's maritime might. Don't miss the sculpture-heavy entrance of the Arsenale; note especially the large ground-level lion sculptures. Carpaccio's series of St George paintings in the Scuola are impressive. Allow half a day to see everything here.

and large lanterns from Venetian flagships and models.

Arsenale
Closed to the public.

The first recorded dockyard in Venice, the **Arsenale Vecchio** dates to about 1104 when the demands of the Crusades stimulated shipbuilding. At one time, 24 boatyards were active. A naval base, depository for arms, and maintenance shop, the Arsenale served as the Venetian State's main shipyard and was enclosed within medieval walls. Its **land entrance** is through a grand Renaissance triumphal arch c.1460; the lions were brought from Ancient Greece (Athens and Piraeus) by Francesco Morosini after his 1687 victory over Morea. The **water entrance**, through which *vaporetti* pass, is marked by two towers rebuilt in 1686.

In the 14C, the Arsenal expanded southeast (**Arsenale Nuovo**). Some 16 000 *marangoni*, men apprenticed as joiners and trained as shipwrights, were employed here and boat-building techniques were highly advanced. During the 15C, the **Arsenale Nuovissimo** was extended north. Destroyed during the 1797 French occupation, the naval complex was rebuilt by the Austrians between 1814 and 1830. The Venetians attacked it in 1848, and the area was abandoned during the third Austrian occupation (1849–66). Restructuring began in the late 19C through to 1914. Among the many shipyard buildings were hemp rope mills, sail lofts and artillery warehouses. Street names recall various other trades and activities: Calle della Pegola (fish), Calle dei Bombardieri (cannonball foundries), Calle del Piombo (lead) and Calle delle Ancore (anchors). Along the canal **Scalo del Bucintoro** (*second on the right after the towers*), designed by **Sanmicheli** (1484–1559), was the dock for the **Bucintoro**, a magnificent state barge built for the Doge by the **arsenalotti**, special artisans. Along the **Galeazzi Canal** is the **Complesso degli Squadratori**, where ship skeletons were squared.

San Francesco della Vigna★
Vineyards were cultivated here when the Franciscans first erected the church in 1534. **Palladio** designed the façade's crowning pediment. The campanile is one of the highest in Venice. Paintings to

see inside are the *Four Evangelists* by **Giovanni Battista Tiepolo**, a *Virgin with Child* by **Veronese** and a *Madonna with Child and Saints* by **Giovanni Bellini**. The tomb of **Doge Marc'Antonio Trevisan** (1553–54) has **Madonna and Child Enthroned★★**, a masterpiece painted in 1450 by the monk **Antonio da Negroponte**.

Scuola di San Giorgio degli Schiavoni★★★

Open year-round Mon 2.45–6pm, Tue–Sun 9.15am–1pm and 2.45–6pm (closed afternoon Sun and hols). €3. 041 52 28 828. Read the panels from the left wall.
The scuola was founded by the Confraternity of the Schiavoni, who traded with the Levant from here. Their patron saints were St George, St Tryphon and St Jerome. **Vittore Carpaccio**'s masterpiece the *Cycle of St George★★★* commemorates the link with the former saint. Other works in the scuola explore the stories of the other two saints.

Sant'Antonin

Dating to the 7C, Sant'Antonin was rebuilt by Longhena. Its mid-17C campanile rises to an Eastern-style cupola.

Campo Bandiera e Moro

Vivaldi was baptised in **San Giovanni in Bràgora★**, a late-15C church which has a copy of a deed confirming his baptism. The highlight is the **Baptism of Christ★★** by Cima da Conegliano (c.1459–1517), but there are also works by **Alvise Vivarini**, Palma il Giovane (1544–1628), Paris Bordone (1500–71) and a truly Gothic *Madonna and Child with St John and St Andrew* (1478) by Alvise's uncle, Bartolomeo Vivarini (1432–c.1491).

San Giorgio dei Greci

Open Mon & Wed–Fri 9am–12.30pm and 2.30–4.30pm, Sat 9am–1pm. 041 52 39 569.
Founded by a colony of Greeks, this complex houses a gently leaning tower, a 16C church and college buildings. A confraternity, the **Scuola di San Niccolò**, was formed here and after the 1453 fall of Constantinople, its numbers increased greatly.
A magnificent **iconostasis★** embellished with holy figures against a gold background screens off the apsed area reserved for the clergy. Wooden stalls are for the congregation during the long Greek Orthodox rites.
Museo di Icone Bizantine-postbizantine – *Open Mon–Sat 9am–2.30pm & 1.30–4.30pm, Sun 10am–5pm. Closed 1 Jan, 25 Dec. €4. 041 52 26 581.www.istituto ellenico.org* – Byzantine and post-Byzantine icons and paintings, exquisite illuminated manuscripts and other artefacts.

©Massimo Pizzotti/age fotostock

San Giorgio dei Greci leaning bell tower

SANTI GIOVANNI E PAOLO★★

This area is striking not only for its majestic architecture but also for the broad range of activity in the district, from the busy commerce of the *calli* between Campo di Santi Giovanni e Paolo and Campo Santi Apostoli, to the tranquillity of Campo dei Gesuiti and the Fondamenta Nuove. From here, the view extends over the choppy waters of the lagoon to the cemetery of San Michele, disturbed only by the passing of the waterbuses.

◈⁓ Walking Tour

Campo di Santi Giovanni e Paolo

The name *Zanipòlo* is a contraction of the names John and Paul in dialect, the two saints to whom the square is dedicated.

Equestrian monument to Bartolomeo Colleoni★★ – The proud gait of Colleoni – a mercenary soldier – his face set with a wilful expression, contrasts powerfully with the restless disposition of the horse.

The commission for such a major monument was awarded to **Verrocchio** by competition. As the master died before it had been cast, Alessandro Leopardi oversaw the project and added the base. Inspiration came from the *Gattamelata* by Donatello in Padua, which is ranked among the highest of its genre.

The decorative **well-head** is attributed to Sansovino, who was also responsible for the side of the Scuola di San Marco that faces onto the canal.

Basilica dei Santi Giovanni e Paolo★★

Open year-round daily 7.30am–6.30pm. 041 52 35 913.

This is the largest church in Venice, founded by Dominican friars late in the 13C, but not consecrated until 1430.

Front – The incomplete façade comprises at ground level a central pointed arch flanked by three blind

Campo di Santi Giovanni e Paolo and Basilica dei Santi Giovanni e Paolo

©Sime/Photononstop

MUST SEE

Vaporetto: Fondamenta Nuove, Cimitero. Neighbouring a large hospital in the northern section of the Castello *sestiere*, the San Zanipòlo district is bounded by the Rio dei Mendicanti and the Fondamenta Nuove. The walking tour below leads into the Cannaregio *sestiere*, and is followed by a tour of the island of San Michele. Don't miss the powerful equestrian statue of Bartolomeo Colleoni. Allow half a day to enjoy this area.

arches; above, the width is divided vertically by plain piers rising up to niches on the roof line with statues of the Dominican Saints.

On either side of the main portal, designed by Bartolomeo Bon, are the two sarcophagi of the Doges Jacopo and Lorenzo Tiepolo.

Interior – The well-lit lofty nave leads to an apse pierced by slender double lancet Gothic windows. In the form of a Latin cross, the church has three aisles and five apses. Huge columns carry great beams that support arches and the cross vaults.

The internal façade commemorates the **Mocenigo Doges**. The **Cappella del Rosario** (Chapel of the Rosary or Lepanto Chapel) was built as a mark of gratitude for the great victory over the Turks. On the walls are depictions by Padovanino and Benedetto Caliari. Opposite the altar, Veronese has painted himself in the guise of the man standing beyond the column. Beyond the apsed chapels on the left, the central apse is replete with **funerary monuments**, holding the remains of several doges.

The first apsidal chapel on the right is dedicated to **Mary Magdalene**. The *Four Evangelists* are frescoed by Palma il Giovane; on the right wall is the monument to the **Sea-Captain Vittor Pisani** (1324–80); on the left is a particularly haunting piece known as *Vanity* or *The Conceited Woman* (17C), depicting a young girl looking at her reflection in a mirror and seeing Death. In the adjacent **Cappella del Crocifisso** (Chapel of the Crucifix), the *Grieving Virgin* and *John the Baptist* are by Alessandro Vittoria.

Before the **Cappella della Madonna della Pace** (Chapel of the Madonna of Peace) stands the **Valier monument** (1705–08), the largest of the Doge monuments. The chapel houses a Byzantine icon and works by Leandro Bassano (*left wall*), Aliense (*right wall*) and Palma il Giovane (*vault*).

In front of the Baroque **Cappella del Beato Giacomo Salomoni** is the tombstone of Ludovico Diedo who died in 1466, a fine example of *niello* engraving. Over the next altar sits an early polyptych by Giovanni Bellini.

The final monument comprises an urn said to contain the skin of Captain Marcantonio Bragadin, who was flayed alive by the Turks in 1571 after the surrender of Famagusta.

Behind the basilica, along Barbaria delle Tole, stands the **Chiesa dell'Ospedaletto**, whose Sala della Musica is open to the public (**guided tours every 30min, Fri–Sat; Apr–Sept 3.30–6.30pm, Oct–Mar 6pm; €3; 041 26 01 974; www.scalabovolo.org**).

SANTI GIOVANNI E PAOLO

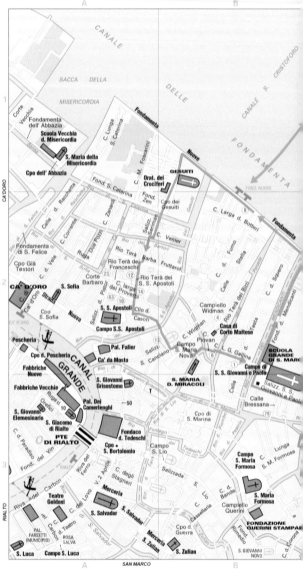

CANALE

SACCA DELLA

MISERICORDIA

CANALE DELLE

CANALE S. CRISTOFORO

FONDAMENTA

FOND. NUOVE

Fondamenta

Nuove

Corte Vecchia
Fondamenta dell' Abbazia
Scuola Vecchia d. Misericordia
S. Maria della Misericordia
Cpo dell' Abbazia

C. Lunga
C. Caterina
C. M. Foscarini

Fond. S. Caterina
Fond. Zen

GESUITI
Orat. dei Crociferi
Cpo dei Gesuiti

C. Larga d. Botteri

Fondamenta

CA'D'ORO

Calle d.
Calle d. Racchetta
C. Corrente
C. Zanardi
C. Pasqualigo

Salizz. Serini

C. Venier
C. d. Fumo
C. d. Stella

C. d. Squero

Rio Fondamenta
di S. Felice
Cpo Già
Testori

Ruga d. Vale

Rio Terà
Sofia
Rio Terà dei
Franceschi
Corte
Barbaro
C. larga
dei Proverbi

Barba
Fruttaroli

(23)
(12)
(14)

Rio Terà dei
S. S. Apostoli

C. d. Biri

Rio Terà Dei Biri

CA' D'ORO
Ca' d'Oro
Strada
Ca'd'Oro
Cpo
S. Sofia
CA'D'ORO
S. Sofia
Nuova

(63) (10)
Salizz.
S. S. Apostoli
Cllo d.
Cason
Campo S.S. Apostoli

Campiello
Widman

C. Widman
Casa di Corto Maltese

Fond. d. Mendicanti

Pescheria

Cpo d. Pescheria Nuova
Fabbriche Nuove
Fabbriche Vecchie

CANAL GRANDE

Pal. Falier

Ca' da Mosto

Salizz.
Canciano

Campo
S. Maria
Nova
Piovan
(13)

C. L. G. Gallina

SCUOLA GRANDE DI S. MARC

Campo di
S. S. Giovanni e Paolo

Salizz. S. S.
Giovanni e Paolo

S. Giovanni Grisostomo

S. Giovanni Elemosinario
S. Giacomo di Rialto

Ruga d.
Oreficì

10

Pal. Dei Camerlenghi

— 50

Fondaco d. Tedeschi

S. MARIA D. MIRACOLI

Calle
Bressana

Cpo di
S. Marina

PTE DI RIALTO

RIALTO

Fond. del
Carbon

Riva del
Ferro

Cpo
S. Bortolomio

C. d. Paradiso

Riva del Carbon

C. d. Carbon

Fond. del Carbon

C. degli
Stagneri

V. 2 Aprile

Fontego

Campo
S. Lio

Tiossi

C. d. Lovo

Salizzada

S. Lio

C. d.
Bande

Teatro Goldoni

Merceria

C. d. Teatro

ROSA
SALVA

S. Salvador

S. Salvador

Casellaria

Campo
S. Maria
Formosa

C. Lunga
S. M. Formosa

S. Maria Formosa

Campiello
Querini

FONDAZIONE QUERINI STAMPAL

PAL.
FARSETTI
(MUNIC(PIO)

S. Luca
Campo S. Luca

Salizz. S. Luca

Merceria

S. Zulian
S. Zulian

Cpo d.
Guerra

Fond.
Rinaldo

S. GIOVANNI
NOVO

C. d. Corona

SAN MARCO

Cimitero

ISOLA
DI S. MICHELE

NOVE

OSPEDALE

Nuove

PEDALE CIVILE

NITI DI VENEZIA

GIOVANNI E PAOLO

Ospedaletto

Barbaria d. Tole

C. d. Cappuccine

C. d. Giustina

di S. Giustina

Fond.

C. Zen

C. S. Francesco

C. del Te Deum

Cpo S. Giustina

Campo di
S. Francesco
della Vigna

**S. FRANCESCO
D. VIGNA**

Cpo d.
Confraternita

Rio di S. Francesco

S. Giovanni
Laterano

Ramo
Capello

S. LORENZO

Salizz. S. Giustina

C. Zorzi

Ponte
S. Francesco

Ramo

S. Lorenzo

Cpo
S. Lorenzo

C. S.
Lorenzo

Corte Nuova

POL

overo

S. Lorenzo

C. d. Lion

C. dei Furlani

Fondamenta
dei Furlani

Campiello
Due Pozzi

**SCUOLA DALMATA
DEI SANTI GIORGIO
E TRIFONE**

S. Giorgio
dei Greci

S. Antonin

N

ARSENAL AND SCHIAVONNI

C

SANTI GIOVANNI
E PAOLO

0 ——————— 150 m

WHERE TO STAY

WHERE TO EAT

STREET INDEX

Scuola Grande di San Marco★

The building provides a façade for Venice's hospital (Ospedaletto) but it is possible to visit the library daily, 8.30am–2pm (except Sat–Sun and public hols). Follow the signs for Biblioteca di San Marco at the far end of the first room, turn right, go upstairs and ring the bell. 041 52 94 323.

This ancient **Scuola**, founded in 1260, was transferred here from its original seat in Santa Croce in 1438. Destroyed in the fire of 1485, it was reconstructed by Lombardo and his sons Antonio and Tullio, before being completed by Lombardo's arch rival, Mauro Codussi. It has reverted to the purpose for which it was founded; at the beginning of the 19C, the building was transformed into a hospital, first for military and now general civic use. At ground level, the **façade** boasts an effective series of *trompe l'oeil* panels; two bold lions guard the left entrance and, to their right, two groups of figures crowd around St Mark healing and baptising Anianus, a cobbler from Alexandria. The **Sala dell'Albergo** now accommodates the medical library and several large pictures, one by Palma il Vecchio and one by Jacopo and Domenico Tintoretto.

Before leaving the room, note the lion with the closed (rather than open) Gospel, often interpreted as a symbol of Venice at war.

The **Sala Capitolare**, also known as the Sala San Marco, has a blue and gold ceiling bearing the symbols of the Scuola. The large panel behind the altar is the work of Palma il Giovane.

Those to each side are by Jacopo and Domenico Tintoretto, as is the one on the opposite wall.

Fondamenta Nuove

The Fondamenta Nuove, which runs alongside the lagoon, was constructed at the end of the 16C. Today waterbuses (*vaporetti*) depart from here for the islands of San Michele, Murano, Burano and Torcello. Venice's main theatre, the **Teatro Fondamenta Nuove**, is to be found near the Sacca della Misericordia.

Gesuiti★

The Jesuit church stands in a peaceful square. It is all the more striking for its white marble Baroque façade, decorated with numerous statues, which include one of the Virgin, to whom it is dedicated, over the pediment. The present building was erected between 1715 and 1729 on the site of the ancient Church of Santa Maria dei Crociferi (1150). The sumptuous interior is enhanced by the white and gold stucco ceiling, the two central sections of which are by Francesco Fontebasso. Over the first altar on the left sits *The Martyrdom of St Lawrence* by Titian; in the left transept is the *Assumption of the Virgin* by Tintoretto. In the sacristy is a cycle of paintings by Palma il Giovane which, among other things, narrates stories from the Bible and of the True Cross.

Oratorio dei Crociferi★

Open Apr–Oct Fri–Sat 3.30–6.30pm. €2. 041 53 22 920. www.scalabovolo.org.

Adjoining the Church of the Jesuits, the Oratory of the Crossbearers dates from the 13C. It was run by the Crutched Friars (*Fratres Cruciferi*), an Order of mendicant friars that was eventually suppressed in 1656. The hospital also served as a refuge for those who had fought in the Crusades. In 1414, it was transformed into a hospice for 12 destitute old ladies. Much of its decoration, on the history of the Crutched Friars, was undertaken between 1583 and 1592 by Palma il Giovane. Included in the painting on the end wall is **Doge Renier Zen**, a principal benefactor of the hospital of Santa Maria dei Crociferi.

On either side of the altar, two paintings depict the foundation of the Order. The three canvases on the left wall illustrate scenes from the life of **Pasquale Cicogna**, Procurator of St Mark's and Doge. Above the doors are represented *The Flagellation* and *The Dead Christ*. In homage to the Virgin, to whom the chapel is dedicated, the ceiling has been decorated with the *Assumption*.

Santa Maria dei Miracoli★
Open Mon–Sat 10am–5pm. Closed 1 Jan, Easter, 15 Aug, 25 Dec. €3. 041 27 50 462. www.chorusvenezia.org.

This exquisite Renaissance church, positioned on the edge of a canal overlooking the small Campo dei Miracoli, recalls the distinctive nature of 14C Tuscan design both in terms of its crisply carved architectural ornament and its marble detailing.

The church is the work of Lombardo, erected to house a miracle-working image of the Madonna by Nicolò di Pietro (1409). In 1489, it was dedicated to the *Immacolata* (the Virgin), the doctrine of the Immaculate Conception having been proclaimed 12 years before this.

The **interior**, especially the barrel vault, resembles a casket. Prophets and patriarchs are depicted in the 50 compartments of the coffered ceiling (*best appreciated with the mirror provided for this purpose*).

Excursion

San Michele in Isola
Venetians and many famous visitors have chosen to be buried here. This great white church – the first Renaissance church in Venice – was designed by Codussi.

The façade includes a fine doorway, topped with a pediment and a statue of the *Madonna*.

The interior extends down to a full set of choir stalls, presided over by St Jerome carved by the Flemish artist, Juste Le Court. Note the fine ceilings.

Cemetery – *Ask for a map at the entrance. Open 7.30am–4/6pm. Closed 7.30am–noon 1 Jan, Easter, 25 Dec.* Here lie Ezra Pound, Igor Stravinsky, Sergei Pavlovich Diaghilev and Josif Brodskij. Condemned for his anti-American propaganda, Ezra Pound, the author of *The Cantos*, was first interned in a concentration camp and then in an asylum, before spending his last years in Italy. He is buried in the Evangelical section to the left on entering. Igor Stravinsky, the Russian composer, along with his associate Sergei Diaghilev, the émigré founder of the Russian Ballet, is buried in the Greek section, at the end.

Also in San Michele Cemetery lie the musician Luigi Nono (1924–90) and the great Goldoni actor Cesco Baseggio (1897–1971).

CA' D'ORO ★★★

Jewel in the crown of the tranquil *sestiere* of Cannaregio, the much photographed Ca' d'Oro with its arches is as symbolic of the city's style and identity as are its gondolas. A visit here, gazing down across the canal onto the Rialto fish market, is a quintessential Venetian experience.

A Bit of History

So luxurious that even the exterior was gilded, this literally was the "House of Gold". Marino Contarini commissioned the construction of his *domus magna* at the beginning of the 15C. The French artist Jean Charlier, known as Zuane de Franza di Sant'Aponal, painted the façade in blue, black and white, and gilded the architectural carving. The original gold may be long gone but the Ca' d'Oro remains the city's gold standard in Venetian Gothic domestic architecture.

Several Lombard masters, followers of Matteo Raverti (active 1385–1436), constructed Ca' d'Oro. Giovanni (c.1360–1442) and Bartolomeo Bon (active 1441–64), the Venetian masters, took over. Bartolomeo, the son of Giovanni, constructed the well-head at the centre of the courtyard. The figures represent the three theological virtues of Fortitude, Justice and Charity. The façade and its reflection in the Grand Canal most captivate today's visitor.

After a long period of restoration, the subdued colours have regained their magical intensity and the delicate marble tracery and crenellation are evident. The façade is harmonious in its asymmetry, despite possible plans for a left wing. The original structure was altered by numerous owners over the course of the centuries. Restoration work started in the 19C, when Prince Troubetskoy bought the Ca' d'Oro as a present for the ballerina Maria Taglioni, but was not faithful to the original construction. At the end of the 19C, more accurate restoration work was undertaken by **Baron Giorgio Franchetti**, who began the gallery that now houses a varied collection of paintings, Renaissance bronze sculpture and medals spanning seven centuries from the 11C to the 18C.

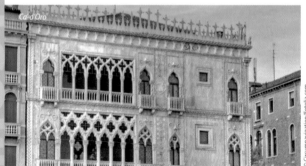
Ca' d'Oro

© Circumnavigation/Fotolia.com

Galleria Giorgio Franchetti

Ca'd'Oro 3932. Cannaregio.
€8. Tue–Sun 8.15am–7pm
(www.cadoro.org).

Veneto-Byzantine art from the 11C to the 13C occupies the first floor. The *Passion* by **Antonio Vivarini** (c.1420–84) is luminous. Also see the English 15C *Scenes from the Passion of St Catherine*.

The gallery's highlight is **Andrea Mantegna**'s uncompleted *St Sebastian*★★. The *memento mori* attached to the candle states *Nihil nisi divinum stabile est – Coetera fumus* (Nothing if not divine is eternal – all the rest is smoke). The wind that has just blown out the candle ruffles St Sebastian's hair. Sebastian surged in popularity during the early Renaissance – perhaps his multiple arrow wounds were as painful as the suffering endured by plague victims. His nude torso gave a painter the opportunity to show his skill in interpreting a sculptural pose. The other saint invoked is the pilgrim San Rocco, traditionally called upon to protect plague victims, here in Venice, from the epidemic. The saint gestures to bubonic swellings that afflict him. Among the bronzes, those of **Pier Giacomo Bonaccolsi** (c.1460–1528) stand out for their Antique style, especially his Apollo. He was official sculptor at the Gonzaga court at Mantua.

See also the *Annunciation*, which appears to be set in Venice itself, and the *Death of the Virgin*, painted by **Vittore Carpaccio** (c.1465–1526) and his studio for the Scuola degli Albanesi. Also worth a look are the *Flagellation* by **Luca Signorelli** (c.1445–1523), two

Seeing Ca' d'Oro
Vaporetto: Ca' d'Oro, San Alvise or Madonna dell'Orto. Cannaregio dominates the northeast side of the Grand Canal, from the Santa Lucia train station, near Ponta della Libertà, east to include the Strada Nuova and the Ca' d'Oro. Don't miss enigmatic St Sebastian by Mantegna in the Ca d'Oro's gallery. Allow half a day to explore this neighbourhood.

vibrant paintings from the *Life of Lucretia* by Biagio d'Antonio (active to 1508), and the *Virgin with Child and St John* by Jacopo del Sellaio (1442–93). The floor above exhibits the *Portrait of the Procurator Nicolò Priuli* by **Tintoretto**; 16C Flemish tapestries; *Venus with a Mirror* by **Titian** (1490–1576); *Portrait of a Gentleman* by **Sir Anthony van Dyck** (1599–1641); *Venus Asleep with her Lover* by **Paris Bordone** (1500–71); and two Venetian scenes by **Francesco Guardi** (1712–93): *St Mark's Square* and the *View of the Wharf towards the Basilica of Santa Maria della Salute*. Frescoes painted by **Giorgione** (c.1476–1510) and Titian for the façades of the **Fondaco dei Tedeschi** are here. Only Giorgione's *Nude* remains; Titian's *Justice* and his great coat of arms are still visible.

Don't miss paintings by Flemish artists, notable for their domestic interiors and landscapes. *The Crucifixion*, by a follower of Van Eyck, shows remarkable detail, particularly in the fortified city that emerges from the background. The Franchetti collection of ceramics is displayed in the adjoining Palazzo Duodo.

CA D'ORO

65

🐚 Walking Tour

The bustling thoroughfare of 🏛 **Strada Nuova** runs almost parallel to the Grand Canal. It is part of the throbbing artery that starts at the Santa Lucia Station, snakes through the Cannaregio *sestiere* and eventually leads to the Rialto. Opened in 1871, the street is vibrant with the uninterrupted flow of people as visitors shuttle to and from the station and the Rialto, and locals do their shopping. It is lined with all sorts of shops, particularly the stretch of Rio Terrà San Leonardo near the station and around the lively market. Fish stalls run the length of the Fondamenta della Pescaria, alongside the Cannaregio Canal.

The **Church of San Felice** houses *St Demetrius with his Follower* by Tintoretto (1518–94). From here, the canal follows the *fondamenta* and emerges in a corner of the city that is rarely frequented by tourists. Time seems to stand still in this peaceful district, which is a world apart from the noise and crowds of the Strada Nuova. Follow the route marked on the map to the **Campo dell'Abbazia**. The centre of this square, paved in brick in a herringbone pattern, is marked by a fine well-head. Bordering on the Rio della Sensa and the Misericordia Canal, the *campo* is hemmed in by the **Church of Santa Maria della Misericordia**, otherwise known as Santa Maria Valverde after the island on which it was built in the 10C, and by the **Scuola Vecchia della Misericordia**. The Baroque façade of the church, the work of Clemente Moli (1651–59), contrasts sharply with the Gothic brick façade of the Scuola of 1451.

Corte Vecchia leads to a viewpoint overlooking the **Sacca della Misericordia**, a cove buffeted by the wind, from where the view stretches into the distance, punctuated only by the Island of San Michele, the tranquil cemetery across the water.

Cross the bridge over Rio dei Muri and pass **Casa del Tintoretto** at no 3399, the house where the artist died in 1594 (a plaque marks the exterior). Turn right onto **Campo dei Mori**; the square's name alludes to the three Mastelli brothers, a family of merchants from Morea in the Peloponnese who settled in Venice in 1112. The name Mastelli was coined after the thousands of *mastelli* (buckets) of gold *zecchini*, or Venetian sequins, they were believed to own. Along the Rio della Madonna dell'Orto stands the brothers' **Palazzo Mastelli del Cammello**.

Next up is the **Madonna dell'Orto★** *(open Mon–Sat 10am–5pm; closed 1 Jan, Easter, 15 Aug, 25 Dec; €3; 041 27 50 462; www.chorusvenezia.org)*, which is known as the Tintoretto Church, as it was the parish church of the Tintoretto family. It was here that Tintoretto was buried. Next to the church stands the **Scuola dei Mercanti**, seat of the Guild of Merchants since 1570, when it transferred itself there from the Frari. Follow the route on the map to **Sant' Alvise★** *(open Mon–Sat 10am–5pm; closed 1 Jan, Easter, 15 Aug, 25 Dec; €3; 041 27 50 462; www.chorusvenezia.org)*, whose simple brick façade is pierced by a rose window and a portal. From here, the route on the map takes you back to Ca d'Oro via the **San Marziale** church.

MUST SEE

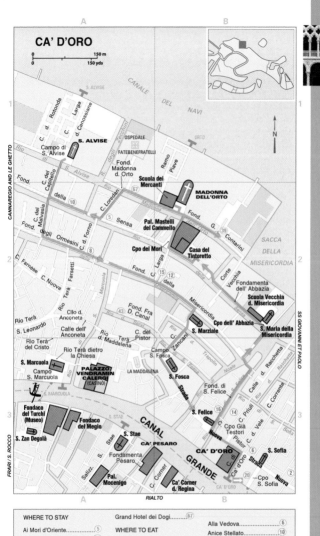

CA' D'ORO

0 ————— 150 m
0 ————— 150 yds

CANNAREGIO AND LE GHETTO

FRARI / S. ROCCO

CANALE DEL NAVI

S. ALVISE

C. d. Rotonda
C. Larga
C. d. Canossiane

Campo di S. Alvise
S. ALVISE

OSPEDALE
FATEBENEFRATELLI

Fond. Madonna d. Orto

C. del Capitello
Fond.
della
Fond.
C. Alvise
(10)
C. Loredan
Sensa
(67)
Scuola dei Mercanti

ORTO

MADONNA DELL'ORTO

Ramo Piave

C. del Malvasia
Fond. degli Ormesini
C. d. Forno
(5)
Sensa
(8)
Pal. Mastelli del Cammello
Fond.
G.
(39)
Contarini

SACCA DELLA MISERICORDIA

C. Farnese
C. Nuova
C. Terà Farsetti
Marcuola
Fond.
C. Larga
della
(15) (12)
Cpo dei Mori
Casa del Tintoretto

Corte Vecchia

Fondamenta dell' Abbazia

Scuola Vecchia d. Misericordia

Rio Terà S. Leonardo
Rio Terà
Cllo d.
(43)
Rio d. Maddalena
Rio Terà del Cristo
Calle dell' Anconeta
Rio Terà dietro la Chiesa
Fond. Fra D. Canal
C. del Pistor
C. Terà
Cpo dell' Abbazia
S. Marziale
S. Maria della Misericordia
Misericordia
C. Zancani
Tragolin

SS GIOVANNI ET PAOLO

S. Marcuola
Campo S. Marcuola
6. MARCUOLA
PALAZZO VENDRAMIN CALERGI (CASINO)
LA MADDALENA
Campo S. Fosca
S. Fosca
Strada
Fond. di S. Felice
Noale
(16)
Fond. di Racchetta
C. Priuli
C. Correnta
C. d. Vale
C. Sofia

Fondaco del Turchi (Museo)
Fondaco del Meglio
S. STAE
CANAL
S. Stae
Salizz.
Stae
C. Corner
CA' PESARO
Fondamenta Pesaro
CA' D'ORO
GRANDE
S. Felice
Nuova
Cpo Già Testori
C. d.
Pistor
(6)
C. di Oro
S. Sofia
Strada
Nuova

S. Zan Degolà
Pal. Mocenigo
Ca' Corner d. Regina
CA' D'ORO
(20)
Cpo S. Sofia
(2)

RIALTO

WHERE TO STAY		
Ai Mori d'Oriente	(5)	
Ca' Sagredo	(20)	
Casa Cardinal Piazza	(39)	
Casa Studentesca Santa Fosca	(43)	

Grand Hotel dei Dogi.........(67)

WHERE TO EAT
Ai Promessi Sposi..............(2)
Al Fontego dei Pescatori....(14)
Al Marinèr........................(8)

Alla Vedova.......................(6)
Anice Stellato....................(10)
Da Rioba...........................(12)
Il Paradiso Perduto............(15)
Vini da Gigio.....................(16)

CA D'ORO

CANNAREGIO
AND IL GHETTO★★

This is the original Ghetto, the first Jewish quarter to be differentiated as such in Western Europe. The term was coined from the word *geto* in Venetian dialect, meaning mortar foundry: the letter g, normally pronounced soft (as in George), was hardened by the first Jews who came from Germany. The busy shops and market around Fondamenta della Pescaria and Rio Terrà San Leonardo contrast with the tranquillity of the squares and the *calli* with their distinctive yellow signs and elegant Hebrew characters.

ᕙᕗ Walking Tour

San Marcuola
The landmark façade of San Marcuola overlooks the Grand Canal. The altars are by Giovanni Morlaiter (1699–1781), who sculpted the high altar in the famous Church of La Salute. See also a *Last Supper* by Tintoretto.

Il Ghetto
The Ghetto **Vecchio** (old) and **Nuovo** (new) are named after the old and new foundries. Jews were first confined to the Ghetto Nuovo – then a practically impenetrable fortified island, when houses were rather squat and low-lying. The area was subjected to a form of curfew at nightfall, after which the drawbridge was raised and the area sealed off. Only in 1866 did access to the Ghetto open and Jews were granted the same rights as other Venetian citizens. Although obliged to stay there, Jews were at least protected.
Confined to this small area, their houses climbed ever taller. Jews were prohibited from undertaking any kind of building work, be it on their houses, their five synagogues, or their *scuole*. Instead, they became *strazzaroli* (dealers in

secondhand clothes and goods), doctors, and bankers involved in moneylending activities: the colours of their stalls were red (*no. 2912*), green and black.

Campo di Ghetto Nuovo
The approach to Campo di Ghetto Nuovo from Calle Farnese might suggest that the area is fortified. From the bridge before the *sottoportego* the evocative view is of unusually tall houses that seem to tower out of the canal. This square recalls the most tragic recent history of the Jews in Venice: a relief commemorates the 204 Jews who were deported from Venice by the Nazis; only eight returned from the death camps. Today the square projects a picture of everyday tranquillity.
Ancient Jewish traditions live on: workshops manufacture objects relating to the Jewish faith, and glass ornaments and cards bear images of rabbis.

🛥 **Museo Ebraico** – *Open Sun–Fri 10am–6/7pm. Guided tours of the synagogues, Sun–Fri hourly from 10.30am; last tour Jun–Sept 5.30pm, Oct–May 3.30pm. Guided tours to the ancient Jewish Cemetery, Spring and Summer*

MUST SEE

Art For Your Sake

Vaporetto: Ferrovia, Ponte delle Guglie, San Marcuola. The Ghetto occupies a corner of the Cannaregio sestiere northeast of the train station near the Cannaregio Canal. The heart of the Ghetto is Campo di Ghetto Nuovo. Don't miss the monumental Palazzo Labia and its attractive square. Allow 3 to 4hrs for a leisurely visit.

Sun 2.30pm. Closed 1 Jan, 1 May, 25 Dec and Jewish festivals. Full tour €8.50; entrance to museum only €3. 041 71 53 59. www.museoebraico.it. The Jewish Museum (which also includes the Ghetto synagogues) has precious artefacts relating to Judaism from decorative objects to ornaments for the sacred scrolls. Of all the Torah covers in the collection, especially precious is that of the Jews encamped, the manna and the hand of Moses issuing forth water from the rock.

Synagogues★★ – Venice's five synagogues occupy the upper floors of various buildings. The **Spagnola** and **Levantina** Synagogues are situated in the Ghetto Vecchio, assigned to the Jews in 1541. The **Tedesca** (Ashkenazi), **Canton** and **Italiana** Synagogues are in Campo di Ghetto Nuovo.

Canal de Cannaregio

To the north, the canal links the lagoon to the Grand Canal. Two bridges cross the Canal; the north bridge closer to the lagoon leads directly to Campo San Giobbe. Continuing toward the Grand Canal, you can reach Ponte Scalzi and the Santa Lucia train station.

San Giobbe

The Old Testament figure of Job is the central theme in this late-15C church begun by Antonio Gambello and completed by Pietro Lombardo. **Doge Cristoforo Moro** (1462–71) is buried here.

Ponte delle Guglie

Further south, the Ponte delle Guglie (1580), Bridge of the Gargoyles, links two main Cannaregio pedestrian routes: **Rio Terrà San Leonardo** to the east, with **Rio Terrà Lista di Spagna** which leads west toward the train station, passing moderately priced cafés, restaurants, bakeries, hotels and coffee bars. This is also a good area to pick up *cichetti* or other treats for a train journey.

Palazzo Labia★★

The ballroom and some state rooms are open to the public by appointment. 041 52 40 782. www.palazzolabia.it.

This late-17C palazzo, built of Istrian stone, takes its name from the wealthy Spanish merchant family who commissioned it. The three façades, adorned with eagles – the family emblem – overlook Campo San Geremia, the Cannaregio Canal and a small square next to the Grand Canal. Venetian nobility had the exclusive prerogative of owning a residence on the Grand Canal. The Labia family, who had paid to be listed in the Libro d'Oro, settled for a view of it.

After the fall of the Republic, Napoleon handed the palazzo to the Austrians. It was neglected until

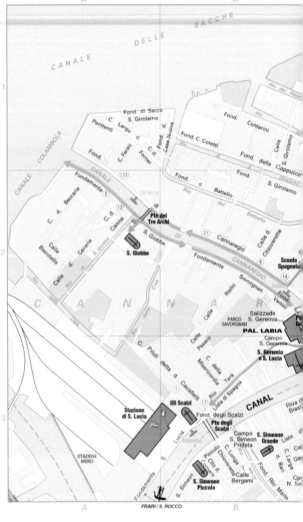

the 1960s when it was bought by the Veneto arm of Italy's national TV network.

San Geremia e Santa Lucia
Bathed in light, the 18C interior holds the remains of Santa Lucia,

a Sicilian martyred under the persecution of Diocletian.
Patron saint of the blind, her Feast Day is the Festival of Lights, which for many Italians – although early – marks the beginning of winter, and in some areas children receive gifts.

CANNAREGIO AND IL GHETTO

```
0          150 m
0          150 yds
```

WHERE TO STAY

WHERE TO EAT

Gli Scalzi

Literally the Church of "the Un-Shod," this was the seat of the Carmelite Order, whose members were obliged to go barefoot (today they wear sandals). The sombre interior shelters the tomb of the last doge, Ludovico Manin.

I FRARI AND SAN ROCCO★★★

The San Rocco area of the San Polo *sestiere* is residential, with fewer tourist magnets. Look for details that give clues to the daily life of modern-day Venetians. San Rocco is an ideal district for a stroll, with interesting monuments and splashes of local colour. Quiet bars and cafés are near the main points of interest, perfect for a break.

A Bit of History

Little is known of **San Rocco** (c.1295–1327), protector of the plague-stricken, other than that he was born in Montpellier in southwest France. Venetian biographer, Francesco Diedo, claims Roch travelled to Italy, where he miraculously cured plague victims (in Aquapendente, Cesena, Mantua, Modena, Parma…) with the sign of the Cross until he, too, was afflicted with the plague in Piacenza but recovered enough to return home. On his way back to Montpellier, he was mistaken for a spy in Angers, incarcerated and died in prison. San Rocco was particularly venerated in Venice, which as a major port was influential in spreading plague epidemics. The Scuole di San Rocco formed in 1478, then was enhanced (to Grande Scuole) in 1485 when the saint's relics were transferred here. The present headquarters was initiated in 1516 by Bartolomeo Bon, who was dismissed in 1524 after a major disagreement with the Scuola leaders. Next entrusted to Scarpagnino, he worked on the building until his death.

The magnificence of the Scuola is in its interior decoration. In 1564, a competition was held for the decoration of the Salla dell'Albergo (a small room on the first floor where the Chapter met). Illustrious artists, including Paolo Veronese, Andrea Schiavone and Federico Zuccari, submitted their drawings, but **Tintoretto** quickly painted a panel for the ceiling and promptly donated his work as a gesture of devotion. The work could not be refused, so Tintoretto went on to furnish the entire Scuola with his paintings.

Spared from Napoleon's edicts, the Confraternity of St Roch is still active today. On 16 August each year, Venice celebrates the saint's day with pomp and circumstance.

ꙮ Walking Tour

San Simeone Piccolo

This is the first eye-catching landmark from the station across Canal Grande. This church with

Seeing I Frari

Vaporetto: S. Tomà, Stazione, Riva di Biasio, S. Stae. Santa Maria Glorioso I Frari is located on the west side of the Grand Canal, in the San Polo *sestiere* not far from the Dorsoduro *sestiere*. San Rocco sits behind I Frari. Don't miss Titian's masterpiece, *Assumption of the Virgin*, in the Maggiore Chapel within the Frari Church, as well as other masterpieces inside. Allow a full day to see everything in this area.

a green dome has a Corinthian *pronaos* (front portico) up a flight of steps. Scalfarotto (c.1700–64) designed this in the tradition of Palladio and Longhena.

San Simeone Grande

Distinct from San Simeone Piccolo, the origins of this church date to 967, with considerable 18C remodelling and an 1861 Neoclassical white façade. The nave and aisles are divided by columns crowned with Byzantine capitals and shrouded in heavy red damask drapes and there is an exquisite *Last Supper* by Tintoretto.

San Zan Degolà

Dedicated to John the Baptist, this church dates to 1007, when the first parish church was built on this site. The early 18C terracotta three-tier façade has a rose window. The harmonious interior has a relief on the right wall that retells the story of John's decapitation.

As with the façade, a harmonious simplicity pervades the interior. The ceiling resembles an inverted ship's hull. Frescoed chapels are at the end of the side aisles.

🦋 Museo di Storia Naturale

Open Tue–Fri 9am–1pm, Sat–Sun 10am–4pm; last admission 30min before closing. Note that several rooms/exhibits are closed while long-term restoration is taking place. Closed 1 Jan, 1 May, 25 Dec. 041 27 50 206. www.msn.ve.it.
The Fondamenta dei Turchi is home to this 13C palace and former Turks' Warehouse, which became the Natural History Museum, after Museo Correr transferred to Piazza San Marco in 1922. Here is the Venice beyond tourist shops,

where nature commands outside the *campi*. Fossils from Bolca, near Verona, show the evolution of vertebrates. See animal species from the lagoon, complete with an enormous crab; learn about the insect world's defence mechanisms, notably that of a giant scorpion. The Dinosaur room has a 3.6m/12 ft-high Ouranosaurus skeleton. Molluscs and minerals include a display of the process of petrifaction. An aquarium showcases lagoon marine life.

San Giacomo dall'Orio★

Open year-round Mon–Sat 10am–5pm. Closed Sun, 1 Jan, Easter, 15 Aug, 25 Dec. €3. 041 27 50 462. www.chorusvenezia.org.
Founded in 976, most of the appearance of this eclectic church dates from 1225. The centre of the main façade features a Veneto-Byzantine patera with a statue of St James the apostle above the portal. By the entrance, the unusual holy water stoop is made of cipolin (onion) marble from Anatolia and the Ionic green marble column is thought to have been brought here from Byzantium. But the church's most striking feature is the Gothic lacunar **ceiling** shaped like an inverted ship's hull.

Of the paintings in the choir stalls attributed to Schiavone, *The Apostles in the Boat* is most likely by him. In the **New Sacristy** are Palma il Giovane's *Crucifixion with the Virgin and St John*; *The Marriage at Cana* also is attributed to him. The **Old Sacristy** (*apply to the custodian*) has fine wood panelling and is decorated with a cycle of paintings by Palma il Giovane.

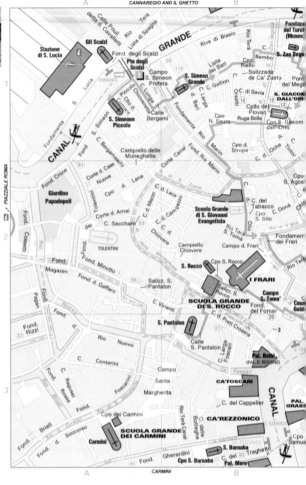

Scuola Grande di San Giovanni Evangelista

Open late Jun–mid-Jul daily 10.30am–7pm, rest of the year by appointment only. Requested donation €5. 041 71 82 34. www.sgiovanniev.it.

The courtyard outside the Scuola of St John the Evangelist is a masterpiece of Venetian Renaissance architecture. The Scuola was the second of the **Scuole Grandi** founded in 1201, and honoured by a confraternity of flagellants who attended religious processions stripped to the waist and whipping themselves with scourges. They are represented in the relief carvings dated 1349

FRARI / S. ROCCO

I FRARI AND SAN ROCCO

at the front, which itself dates from 1454, when the large ogee windows were inserted. The double stairway inside, lit by large arched windows, was built by Codussi. On the first floor, the oval windows were added by Giorgio Massari (1727), who raised the height of the **salone**. Various craftsmen are responsible for the decoration on the ceiling and the walls, including Tintoretto and Pietro Longhi. The *salone* adjoins the Oratory of the Cross, built to house Carpaccio's cycle of the *Miracles of the Relic of the True Cross,* now in the Accademia.

Campo dei Frari

In early medieval times, this swampy area was home to a Benedictine Abbey, then the Franciscans were given the property and conducted a major land reclamation that resulted in what is now a prestigious neighbourhood anchored by one of Italy's most splendid churches.

Church of Santa Maria Gloriosa dei Frari★★★

Open daily, 9am (1pm Sun)–6pm (last admission 5.45pm). Closed 1 Jan, Easter, 15 Aug, 25 Dec. €3. 041 27 50 462. www.chorusvenezia.org.
This great Italian Gothic church is known as the Frari, an abbreviation of Fra(*ti Mino*)ri – the first order of Franciscan friars. It is frequently compared to the Church of Santi Giovanni e Paolo for its scale and style. Monumental in stature, it is flanked by the second-tallest campanile (70m/229ft 6in) after St Mark's.Strikingly magnificent, its massive architecture is articulated with fine detail; Franciscan yet very

original. Every angle impresses. The best view of the apses is from the Scuola di San Rocco (opposite), or from the bridge built by the monks in 1428, its late-Gothic tripartite façade a masterpiece of design.
Interior – Constructed in the form of a Latin cross, the nave is divided from the aisles by 12 huge cylindrical piers that soar up to the criss-cross of timber beams that underpin the vaulted ceiling. The floor tiles are from Verona.
The art is as spectacular as the architecture. The first noteworthy monument (*left aisle*) is Neoclassical and dedicated to **Canova** (1757–1822) (1), originally designed by the sculptor to commemorate Titian. Figures before the pyramid represent Sorrow (portrait of Canova) with Venice (left), in the company of Sculpture (heavily veiled), Painting and Architecture. Canova was esteemed not only for his art, but for tirelessly and skilfully negotiating the return of works of art seized by Napoleon. Beyond the Baroque monument to **Doge**

Church of Santa Maria Gloriosa dei Frari

©Stefano Brozzi/age fotostock

Giovanni Pesaro is the **Madonna di Ca'Pesaro Chapel**, dominated by Titian's altarpiece.

Serving as a glorious harbinger of the Maggiore Chapel and Titian's *Assumption* are 124 **choir stalls** beautifully inlaid with 15C Venice scenes. The two organs on the right are signed Gaetano Callido (1794) and Giovanni Piaggia (1732) respectively. Beyond, early 17C paintings by Andrea Micheli, known as Vicentino, illustrate the *Works of Corporeal Mercy* (*left*) alongside his *Creation of the World*, the *Brazen Serpent*, a *Last Judgement* and the *Glory of Paradise* (*right*).

In the left transept, the first chapel on the left is the St Mark's or Corner Chapel, which houses the *Triptych of St Mark* by Bartolomeo Vivarini (c.1432–91). High up on the wall opposite is *Christ's Descent into Limbo* by Jacopo Palma il Giovane. The **Maggiore Chapel** is the focal point of the magnificent perspective of the Frari Church. All points converge on Titian's **Assumption of the Virgin**, which was commissioned by the Franciscans in 1516. This major work, the first religious subject undertaken by the painter, caused the friars some consternation. Instead of Mary's restful contemplation, the crowded painting shows the Apostles disturbed by the mystery of this supernatural event; *putti* and winged angels, singing and playing music, emphasise the upward movement of the composition. The brilliance of heaven contrasts with the realms of shadow and darkness on earth, even as bright light pushes the figure of the Virgin into bold perspective.

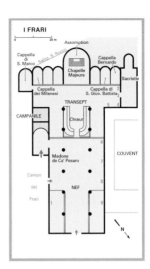

Against the presbytery walls are two funerary monuments, one to **Doge Nicolò Tron** and the other to **Doge Francesco Foscari**. **Donatello**'s only Venetian work and the jewel of the Chapel of John the Baptist shows *John the Baptist* with the index finger of his right hand raised against Herod as a sign of admonition (unfortunately the finger is missing). Beyond the former Santissimo Chapel, now dedicated to Maximilian Kolbe, comes the Bernardo Chapel containing a Polyptych by Bartolomeo Vivarini (1482). Other notable features include the equestrian monument to Paolo Savelli (2); the monument to Benedetto Pesaro (3); the terracotta monument to the Blessed Peacemaker of the Frari (4); the monument to Jacopo Marcello (5); the sacristy's triptych by Giovanni Bellini; the chapel of St Catherine of Alexandria (6); the statue of St Jerome, (7); the altar of Purification (8); and Titian's Mausoleum (9).

Casa di Goldoni

Open Thu–Tue 10am–5pm (4pm Nov–Easter). Closed 1 Jan, 1 May, 25 Dec. €2.50. 041 27 59 325. www.museicivicveneziani.it.
Carlo Goldoni was born in this palazzo. He later abandoned his life as an affluent lawyer and became a famous playwright. The palazzo and its small courtyard, complete with a well and staircase, is home to the International Institute for Theatrical Research, including a puppet theatre, housing works by Goldoni and Pietro Longhi.

Campo San Tomà

This lovely square with its simple, now deconsecrated 10C church was remodelled in 1742. The **Scuola dei Calegheri** was acquired by the guild of cobblers in the 15C.

Scuola Grande di San Rocco

Open 28 Mar–2 Nov 9am–5.30pm; rest of the year 10am–5pm. Closed 1 Jan, Easter Sun, 25 Dec. €7; no charge 16 Aug (St Rocco's feast day). 041 52 34 864. www.scuolagrandesanrocco.it.
Often used as a concert hall, the **interior★★★** of this Scuola is decorated with works by artists like Giannantonion Pellegrini and Tintoretto. The ground floor windows of the Scuola Grande are early Venetian Renaissance, while those above are Mannerist in design. The rear façade aces the canal, its simpler portico has finely carved details (note the heads on the pilasters on the first floor).

San Rocco

The present late 18C façade of this church (*open Mon–Sat 7.30am–2.30pm & 3–5pm. Sun and hols 8am–12.30pm & 3–5pm*) has statues of the *Saints* and the *Blessed* by Marchiori and the Austrian-born Gianmaria Morlaiter.

Above the entrance door, the **old organ door panels** painted by Tintoretto depict *The Annunciation* and *The Presentation of St Roch to the Pope*. In the first side chapel of the left aisle, the altarpiece is by Sebastiano Ricci; the two tall panels by Pordenone show *St Martin* and *St Christopher*, and the panel below, *Christ Chasing the Moneychangers from the Temple*, is by Fumiani. Over the second altar is an *Annunciation and Angels* by Solimena. Four canvases by **Tintoretto** are in the presbytery, with two more hanging between two altars.

San Pantalon

Despite its unfinished façade (1668–86), this church recalls others in Venice such as San Marcuola and San Lorenzo. It houses an undisputed masterpiece by Fumiani comprising 60 canvas ceiling panels illustrating *The Martyrdom and Glory of St Pantaleone*, executed 1684–1704, and restored in 1970. This tour de force of perspective projects the nave high into the sky.

The presbytery decoration is by the same artist, often called *fumoso* (meaning smoky) because of his predilection for dark colours, is characteristic of a period tormented by ever-present death. To the left of the high altar, the small chapel, dedicated to a relic of the True Cross, houses *Paradise* (1444) by Antonio Vivarini. In the third chapel on the right is a work by **Veronese**.

I CARMINI ★

The Dorsoduro district is a lively mix of university life with the daily markets in the Campo Santa Margherita and along the Rio di San Barnaba. Waterborne greengrocers sell the freshest produce, including delicate artichoke hearts. Enjoy the eateries catering to students and tourists, or stop in at a quintessentially Italian bar. Many shops cater to locals rather than visitors and, between San Barnaba and Campo di Santa Margherita, the odd authentic *bottega* sells carvings and masks.

✿. Walking Tour

Campo Santa Margherita

Scuola dei Varoteri (Confraternity of Tanners) and the stunted campanile of the former **Church of Santa Margherita** distinguish this large *campo*. Cafés, shops and market stalls add a buzz. Its position alongside the **Rio della Scoazzera** (meaning sewage channel), now running underground, accounts for its humble appearance, which nobility preferred to avoid when building patrician *palazzi*.

Scuola Grande dei Carmini ★

Open Apr–Oct daily 9am–6pm (Sun 4pm), Nov–Mar daily 9am–4pm. Closed 1 Jan, 25 Dec. €5. 041 52 89 420.

Scuola dei Carmini (Guild of Dyers), devotee of the Virgin of Carmelo, sits at the narrowest end of the Campo di Santa Margherita. Inside, the decoration includes panels by **Giovanni Battista Tiepolo**.

I Carmini

The simple Renaissance façade of this church and its 14C portico are in stark contrast to the rich decoration of the interior. Dark 17C and 18C paintings and the heavy black and gold of the statues lend a lugubrious atmosphere; yet the brightness of the internal space, the 14C woodwork, and its many paintings, soften the initial impression. Interesting works of art: (*left aisle, near the entrance*) Padovanino's *San Liberale Saves Two Men Condemned to Death* and *St Nicholas between John the Baptist and Saint Lucy with Angels* by Lorenzo Lotto; (*right wall*) *Feeding of the Five Thousand* by Palma il Giovane; (*above the fourth altar, right aisle*) *Presentation of Christ in the Temple* by Tintoretto. Many of the paintings were restored by funds from the American Committee to Rescue Italian Art.

San Nicolò dei Mendicoli

The *Mendicoli* alludes to the beggars who lived in the area, notably the *pinzochere* (impoverished religious women) who sheltered in the portico. Probably founded in the 7C, this building mostly dates to the 12C, as does the massive belltower. The façade and its portico echo those of the Church of San Giacomo di Rialto. Inside, the wooden statuary dates to the 16C. Paintings by followers of Veronese (1528–88) depict *Episodes from the Life of Christ*.

Anzolo Rafael

The **Church of Angelo Raffaele** shows the *Stories of Tobias and the Angel* purportedly by Gian'Antonio

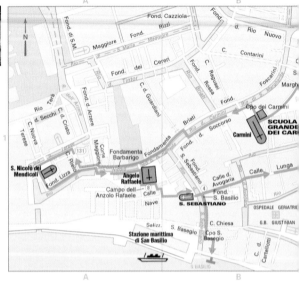

Guardi (1699–1760) on the parapet of the organ. Calle Nave branches off to the left towards the Church of St Sebastian.

San Sebastiano★★
Open Mon–Sat 10am–5pm.
Closed 1 Jan, Easter, 15 Aug,
25 Dec. €3. 041 27 50 462.
www.chorusvenezia.org.
The true beauty of this church lies in its rich internal decoration: Vasari described Veronese's paintings as "joyous, beautiful and well-conceived".

See the individual masterpieces and then enjoy the overall effect. Next to the organ, the **bust of Veronese** marks the burial site of the master painter who celebrated the beauty of the world with depictions of luxurious silk and velvet, buxom women in flesh and stone, surrounded by gold, glass and silver. The opulent quality of his art renders the Church of St Sebastian unique; this painter was occupied with the cycle of frescoes for the most significant part of his life.

Seeing I Carmini

Vaporetto: Ca'Rezzonico, San Tomà or San Basilio. South of the Grand Canal, the Dorsoduro neighbourhood sweeps west from La Salute to the Canale Scomenzera, encompassing the **Zattere** promenade along the Giudecca canal. Don't miss Ca'Rezzonico, an outstanding palazzo, exquisitely furnished. If you have time to see only one palazzo, this is the one. Allow about half a day, plus 2hrs for Ca'Rezzonico. Children will enjoy watching the constant parade of all manner of watercraft on the Giudecca canal, including massive cruise ships.

St Sebastian recurs in many of the frescoes: the saint is shown pierced by arrows from archers and his martyrdom is depicted.

🍃 Campo San Barnaba

Calle Lunga San Barnaba boasts few important sights but has the feel of authentic neighbourhood Venice. It is lined with friendly eating places, paint shops and a model-maker's shop selling intricate miniatures.

The buzz of the popular Campo San Barnaba is generated by both tourists and locals. There are small shops, cafés and food stalls along the Rio di San Barnaba near the Ponte dei Pugni.

Ca' Rezzonico★★

This palazzo, the last designed by **Baldassare Longhena**, offers full immersion into the Venetian noble's life. Henry James (1843–1916) considered the Ca' Rezzonico to be so majestic as to be almost mythological; Ruskin (1819–1900), who detested the Baroque style, likened the pilasters to "piles of cheese". Originally commissioned for the Bon family, ownership was transferred to a family from Lake Como; one of its progeny was to become Pope Clement XIII (1758). Ca' Rezzonico was once owned by **Robert Browning** (1812–89) and his wife, the poet Elizabeth Barrett (1806–61), before passing to their son Robert (1849–1913). Robert Browning Jr. sold the palazzo in 1906 when his divorce obliged him to return a dowry.

Ca' Rezzonico now houses the **Museo del Settecento Veneziano** *(Museum of 18C Venice; open Easter Sat–early Nov Wed–Mon 10am–6pm (5pm early Nov– Easter). Last admission one hour before closing. Closed 1 Jan, 1 May,*

25 Dec. €6.50. 041 24 10 100;
www.museicivicivenezianiti.it).
Your visit begins at an enormous
staircase, designed to impress
guests and host elaborate Carnival
fancy-dress parties. The *Salone
da Ballo* (ballroom) is dominated
by the great coat of arms of the
Rezzonico family and frescoed by
Giambattista Crosato. Early-18C
Venetian pieces include the ebony
figurines and delicate chairs that
once belonged to the Venier family.
In spring, classical music concerts
are staged here.

The ceiling of *Sala dell'Allegoria
Nuziale* was frescoed by Tiepolo in
1757 for the society wedding of
Ludovico, one of the members of
the Rezzonico family. The *Sala dei
Pastelli* (Pastel Room) has portraits
by Rosalba Carriera (1675–1757),
while in the *Sala degli Arazzi*
(Tapestry Room) 17C Flemish
tapestries tell the story of Solomon
and the Queen of Sheba.

The *Sala del Trono* (Throne Room)
features the majestic golden throne
adorned with nymphs, sea horses
and *putti* used by Pope Pius VI on
his visit to Venice in 1782. Other
ground floor rooms include the

Sala del Tiepolo (Tiepolo Room),
Sala del Lazzarini and *Sala del
Brustolon*.

Upstairs are the *Sala del Clavi-
cembalo* and *Sala del Parlatorio*
(Parlour Room). Chinoiserie
predominates in the *Sala delle
Lacche Verdi* (Green Lacquer Room),
while Guardi paintings hang in *Sala
del Guardi*. The spacious *Pinacoteca
Egidio Martini* houses a collection of
paintings from the Venetian School
dating from the 15C–20C. The visit
concludes with a reconstruction of
the *"Ai Do San Marchi"* pharmacy.

Ca' Foscari

A famous example of the Gothic
style, Ca' Foscari was built in 1452
for the Doge Francesco Foscari.
Today it accommodates the
headquarters of the **University of
Venice**. The approach from Calle
Foscari is not ideal, as the view
of the palazzo is restricted by the
crenellated wall that surrounds the
courtyard. Bustling with student
activity, Ca' Foscari is best seen
from the Grand Canal which, in
turn, may be glimpsed from the
salone on the ground floor, which
periodically hosts **exhibitions**.

Ca' Rezzonico

LA GIUDECCA

La Giudecca was once dotted with the villas of wealthy nobles. Today, the prestigious Cipriani and the old factory converted into the Molino Stucky Hilton recall its luxurious past. The *ferro* (metal ornamentation) on the prow of every gondola has six metal teeth representing the six *sestieri*, while the seventh tooth on the other side represents the island of Giudecca, separated from the other *sestieri* by the Giudecca Canal. Giudecca is a quiet haven for visitors who seek a relaxed and peaceful atmosphere. The island's name may be a reference to the Jews (*giudei*) who once lived here, or to the 11C *zudegà* (judgement) that guaranteed land to noble families who had been exiled from elsewhere.

Walking Tour

Molino Stucky

Reminiscent of Dickens' London, this late-19C work is named after the Swiss entrepreneur who commissioned it. The factory has been transformed into **Hilton Molino Stucky Venice**, with Venice's first rooftop hotel pool.

Sant'Eufemia

This is the oldest church on the island, dating to the 9C and still graced with 11C Veneto-Byzantine capitals. Inside, works by Bartolomeo Vivarini (c.1432–91) and Giambattista Canal (1745–1825) inspire.

Il Redentore★

Open Mon–Sat, 10am–5pm. Closed 1 Jan, Easter, 15 Aug, 25 Dec. €3. 041 27 50 462. www.chorusvenezia.org.
In 1576 Venice was decimated by the plague, which had raged for more than a year. **Doge Alvise Mocenigo** proposed that a new church be dedicated to the Redeemer, and every year thereafter honoured by a solemn procession. **Palladio** was commissioned to design the church and sought to make it fulfil its votive function above all else. Its longitudinal axis was necessary for the long procession of clergy and dignitaries. The flat Classical façade was inspired by biblical descriptions of Jerusalem's Temple.

Le Zitelle

The **Church of Santa Maria della Presentazione** was also designed by **Palladio**. The name *Zitelle* refers to the girls accommodated in the adjoining hospice who earned their keep making lace.

Seeing La Giudecca

Vaporetto: Zitelle, Redentore, Giudecca, S. Eufemia. Laid out in the shape of a fishbone, the eight islands that make up Giudecca justify its original name: Spinalonga (long spine). **Don't miss** a long meander along the *fondamenta* following the canals that divide the island into its eight parts, from Molino Stucky (factory turned luxury hotel) east towards the Church of San Giorgio Maggiore. Allow 30–45min for the walk and visit to Il Redentore. Then stop in the **Hotel Cipriani** or Harry's Dolci for lunch or afternoon tea; it's advisable to make advance reservations.

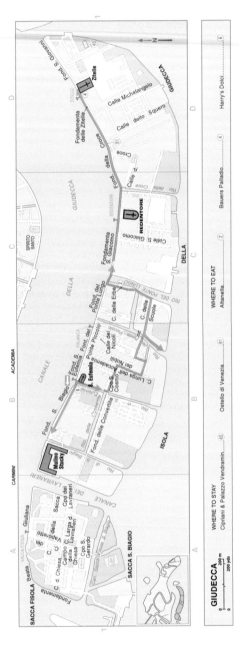

GIUDECCA

0	200 m
0	200 yds

SAN GIORGIO MAGGIORE★★

The island of San Giorgio Maggiore is not only thoroughly Venetian but provides first-rate views over the city. No bars or restaurants encourage visitors to linger for long, but it is a "must" for a unique view of Venice, for those seeking serenity, and for Palladio fans.

A Bit of History

The island's name relates to a church erected here in 790; the term *maggiore* is used to distinguish it from another island, San Giorgio in Alga. The island's history has been associated with the Benedictine order since 982 when a monastery was founded here. Favoured by the doges, on 26 December they would attend Mass in celebration of the Feast of St Stephen. The island's decline coincided with that of the Republic of Venice. After both Napoleon and the Austrians had defiled the artistic beauty of the island, its finest buildings continued to be devastated by various armies, including the Italian army, which used the dormitory for storage during the Second World War. The island's restoration to its former beauty is largely due to the Cini Foundation and to the Benedictine monks who remain the sole inhabitants. It is a place of retreat and deep religious faith. The monastery is the only place to stay, eat or drink here.

🐾 Walking Tour

San Giorgio Maggiore★
Open May–Sept 9.30am–12.30pm and 2.30pm–6.30pm (4.30pm rest of the year). Church free, campanile €3. 041 52 27 827.

Palladio designed the current church, whose rebuilding began in 1566. The front is dominated by a great triangular pediment supported by four columns, suggesting a Classical temple. The interior is bright with a vaulted ceiling. In the third chapel, *The Martyrdom of SS Cosmas and Damian* was painted by **Jacopo Tintoretto**, who also did the two large paintings in the presbytery. The main altar features late-16C sculptures by Gerolamo and Giuseppe Campagna. The door to the right leads into the chapel (*open for Sunday services only*), decorated with Tintoretto's final work, *Deposition from the Cross*. The 1726 appearance of the **campanile**, by Scalfarotto, offers a classic **view★★★** over Venice.

Seeing San Giorgio Maggiore

Vaporetto: S. Giorgio. In St Mark's Basin near the entrance to the Giudecca Canal, San Giorgio faces Piazza San Marco, a small island with prime real estate in terms of exposure. Its glorious church of the same name is generally the first head-turner for travellers arriving in the city by water. **Don't miss** the best possible view of Venice, from the church's belltower. Take a bottle of water as there are no refreshment facilities. Budget accommodation is available in the monastery, call 041 52 27 827. The proposed tour takes about 2hrs.

S. GIORGIO MAGGIORE

Campo S. Giorgio

S. GIORGIO

S. GIORGIO MAGGIORE

Fondazione Giorgio Cini

CANALE

Fond. S. Giovanni

DELLA

TEATRO VERDE

GRAZIA

GIUDECCA

SALUTE

N

Fondazione Giorgio Cini

Housed in a beautifully restored Benedictine monastery, this private institution restores many of Venice's monuments, and stages important international conventions.

The foundation was conceived by **Vittorio Cini** (1885–1977), a man who showed great courage and philanthropy during his life as a financier and government minister.

Library★ *The entrance to the library is off the first cloisters and up the main staircase on the right. Guided tours (1hr) Sat–Sun 10am–4.30pm. €12. 041 52 89 900. www.cini.it.* Designed by Longhena, the library has carved wooden figures and a 17C Mannerist ceiling. Antique furnishing and objets d'art on the *piano nobile* (first floor) re-create the building's original character. Some thirty paintings of the Tuscan School are displayed, as well as ceramics, porcelain, ivory caskets and badges, enamels, gold-work, candle-sticks, chandeliers made in Murano, terracotta sculptures and furniture.

Cloisters – The first cloister, the Chiostro dei Cipressi (Cypress cloister), was designed by Palladio; it leads into the Teatro Verde, an open-air theatre with marble seats. The second cloisters are older, once known as the Chiostro degli Allori (Laurel Chloister). Veronese worked with Palladio on the Refectory (*Refettorio*); his *Wedding at Cana* was removed by Napoleon; it now hangs in the Louvre.

Dormitorio – The dormitory building is impressive for its sheer size (128m/420ft long) and lightness. Known as the *manica lunga*, meaning the "long sleeve", it affords fine views towards the Riva degli Schiavoni.

MUST SEE

SANT'ELENA E SAN PIETRO ★

The Sant'Elena and San Pietro districts of the Castello *sestiere* are peaceful yet often vibrant. Their green spaces, a novelty in Venice, are popular with locals. The view from the public gardens and the Park of Remembrance over the lagoon and St Mark's Basin is magnificent. Movement and activity pervade the area around the Rio di Santa Anna with its floating market, and extend to the bustling commercial activities of the only street (*via*) in Venice to be named as such, Via Garibaldi.

Isola di Sant'Elena

Up until the 11C, the island was known as a *cavana* (refuge), with sheltered anchorage for boatmen and fishermen. Relics of St Helen (c.257–336), mother of the Emperor Constantine, are housed in the church (first chapel on the right) and were brought to Venice in 1211, after the Fourth Crusade. The small monastery, established in 1060, was built by Benedictine monks from Tuscany in 1407, with later rebuilding from 1439 to 1515. During Napoleon's rule, the monastery was disbanded and its assets sold and dispersed; the church was used as a warehouse and troops were billeted in the convent buildings. During the late-19C and early 20C, the area around the church and monastery was extended and urbanised.

Today, the church and convent accommodate Servite monks. This quarter is one of the cheapest parts of the city to dine out; places for a pizza or a particularly inexpensive *menu a prezzo fisso* (set-price meal) proliferate.

Church

On the far side of the Rio di S. Elena rises the Church of Sant'Elena, flanked by a stadium and military base. The Gothic façade on its portal (1467) has a sculptural group by Antonio Rizzo, which shows the Capitano da Mar (Sea Captain-General), **Vittore Cappello**, kneeling before St Helen.

Parco delle Rimembranze

This Park of Remembrance is dedicated to soldiers who lost their lives in the Second World War. Children's play areas, plenty of green space and a skating rink make it a popular place for families on a sunny day.

Biennale

See Must Do. The exhibition has always been held in the Giardini Publicci, where the pavilions of the various countries which elect to exhibit here have been erected, and expands to various *palazzi* and other sites around Venice. Held every odd-numbered year between June and November, visit www.labiennale.org.

Chiesa San Giuseppe

Beyond Viale Trento in a little square is the 16C church dedicated to St Joseph. See *St Michael and Lucifer Fighting over the Soul of Michele Bon* by Jacopo (1518–94) and Domenico (c.1560–1635) Tintoretto.

SANT'ELENA E SAN PIETRO

Vaporetto: S. Elena, Giardini Biennale. In the Castello Gardens stand the Biennale pavilions. This area is the eastern extremity of the Castello *sestiere*, separated from the rest of the lagoon by the green space of the Park of Remembrance. Sant'Elena is quiet and, unusually for Venice, devoid of canals. The small island of San Pietro lies just north. Don't miss Viale Garibaldi, a long pathway through a tree-shaded expanse lined with charming homes, from where even here huge ships seem very close and side streets and canals are likely to be criss-crossed with laundry. Allow 3hrs for a leisurely visit.

Isola di San Pietro di Castello

Inhabited before Venice was founded, this island was known as **Olivolo**, perhaps after its olive groves. The *sestiere* commemorates a castle (hence the name Castello) that was either built or found there by the earliest Venetians. Since time immemorial, it has been the religious symbol of the city. The basilica stands in an open, grassy area, the venue for lively celebrations during the Feast of San Pietro di Castello. It shelters the body of the first Patriarch of Venice.

San Pietro di Castello★

Mon–Sat 10am–5pm. Closed 1 Jan, Easter, 15 Aug, 25 Dec. €3. 041 27 50 462. www.chorusveneiza.org.

The Church of St Peter at Castello was regarded as Venice's official cathedral until 1807, before which St Mark's was merely considered to be the doge's chapel. Erected in the 8C on the foundations of a church that dates to 650, the façade conforms to Palladian design. On the right is the former late-16C Patriarchal Palace. The nearby campanile leans to one side.

MUST SEE

IL LIDO

The Lido is Venice's seaside resort. A once sophisticated and avant-garde tourist beach development, it is now looking a little run down. For many visitors Il Lido is forever associated with the legacy of Luchino Visconti's *Death in Venice*, which was filmed at the Hotel des Bains, and haunted by the disconcerting yet majestic Hotel Excelsior, so reminiscent in style and sheer boldness of Ludwig of Bavaria's castle in Neuschwanstein. The Lido plays host to the glittering Venice International Film Festival every September, when film directors, actors and critics meet, accompanied by their inevitable jet-setting entourage and crowds of curious onlookers *(see Must Do)*.

⛵ Venice International Film Festival

The world's first film festival was inaugurated in 1932 at the Hotel Excelsior on the initiative of Conte Volpi di Misurata and Luciano De Feo, Secretary General of the International Institute of Cinematographic Art. The **Festival of International Cinematographic Art** was more of an exhibition of the art of cinematography than a review, organised to complement the Biennale.

The festival's top prize is the Golden Lion (Leone d'Oro) award. Most of the films that have won are small-budget arthouse productions that have remained anonymous to the film-going public at large, although there are exceptions in recent years.

⛵ Gran Viale Santa Maria Elisabetta and the Beach

The Lido's main thoroughfare stretches from the *vaporetto* stop to the Piazzale Bucintoro (*accessible by bus*), which leads to Lungomare Guglielmo Marconi. This area is home to some of the best hotels, with their colourful beach huts along the seafront. The Casino and the headquarters of the Cinema Festival are also located here.

Jewish Cemetery

Opening times call 041 71 53 59. www.museoebraico.it.

At the north end of the island, the old Jewish Cemetery dates back to 1389.

Seeing Il Lido

Extending roughly north–south to the east of Venice, the Lido resembles a long, thin leg of land (12km/7.5mi long and around 1km/0.6mi wide), fronting the Adriatic Sea. The sandy stretch serves as a barrier island for the Venetian lagoon and a beach for Venetian residents. It is easy to get to the Lido: hop onto *vaporetto* line 1, 82 or N from Piazza San Marco and half an hour later you will arrive at Santa Maria Elisabetta. **Don't miss** the beach in summer or any time, as to understand Venice you also need to get a sense of the sea. Sunbathers beware that the best stretches are privately owned.

Allow a couple of hours soaking in the sights and sounds. Cycling is the best way to explore this island, which along with the beach is fun for kids. You can connect by bus or bike to the islands south of the Lido.

MURANO★★

From the water, Murano's lighthouse is its most distinctive symbol. The island appears to be walled-in by its long line of furnaces. As you step off the *vaporetto*, you will be urged, even cajoled, to visit the glassworks, and while the commercial aspect of the "invitation" can be irritating, it is well worth watching the various stages and processes. Look for glassmakers that operate only on this island and sell only their own wares, as unfortunately cheap knockoffs are at prices that appeal to tourists, but may be for glass not made on this continent. If you need a rest, see the island from a *vaporetto*. The circular tour goes through the centre of Murano, making frequent stops, including the museum. This is especially nice late afternoon, when most tourists have gone, children are coming home from school and the inhabitants are going about their workaday life.

A Bit of History

By the end of the 13C, glassmaking was so widespread in Venice that the threat of fire ravaging the city was ever constant. Countless small fires frequently broke out due to the widespread use of wood and candles; had these incidents not been contained, fire would have spread quickly, with disastrous consequences. Finally, three nervous centuries later, the Grand Council moved the glassworks away from the city to Murano, ensuring the safety of the city and the protection of the Venetian glassblowers' secrets. The origins of glass may be rooted in the ancient Orient where potters learned how glass was formed from silicon sand when glazing their ceramics by firing them in a kiln. The process was already in widespread use by the time the books of Job and Proverbs were written, as recorded in the Bible, and commonly practised in Egypt by the 4th millennium BC, as small objects found in datable tombs demonstrate. The colours blue and green were created by the addition of copper and cobalt oxide. The technique for blowing glass, however, as favoured by the Romans, came later.

In 1203, following the occupation of Constantinople, Venice secured

The island of Murano in the lagoon

MUST SEE

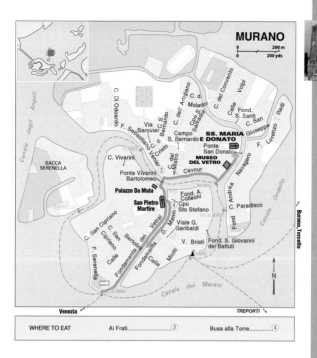

0   200 m
0   200 yds

Canale degli Angeli

C. Di Oboardo

C. dell' Artigiano

C. d. Molado

C. del Convento

Volpi

Fond. S. Santi

C. San Giuseppe

F. Lorenzo Radi

Via Barovier

F. Sebastiano Venier

C. O. d. Bernardo

Cpo Salvati

Campo S. Bernardo

SS. MARIA E DONATO

Ponte San Donato

MUSEO DEL VETRO

C. Vivarini

Ponte Vivarini Bartolomeo

Cavour

F. D. Cristo

C. dal Cristo

SACCA SERENELLA

Palazzo Da Mula

San Pietro Martire

Fond. A. Colleoni

Cpo Sto Stefano

C. Paradisco

C. San Cipriano

C. San Cipriano

Calle

Bertolini dei Vetrai

D. Manin

Viale G. Garibaldi

Fond Andrea Navagero

Canale Ondello

Burano, Torcello

F. Serenella

Fondamenta

Fondamenta

Calle

Miotti

V. Briati

Fond. S. Giovanni dei Battuti

COLONNA

FARO

N

Venezia

Canale dei Marani

TREPORTI

WHERE TO EAT	Ai Frati..........................②	Busa alla Torre...............④

the "exclusive" collaboration of immigrant potters in exchange for preferential treatment from the Republic. However, the terms of agreement were ruthless; if the glassmakers refused to return to the city, they were hunted down and killed. Venice's supremacy in glassmaking remained uncontested until the end of the 16C.

Venice and Murano have long lost their monopoly on the industry, but even today, modern glass creations from Murano are considered works of art.

Within everyone's budget are the *murrine*, which sparkle with colour, often set into costume jewellery, and the distinctive discs of kaleidoscopic patterns. The final effect of this unique glassworking technique is achieved by juxtaposing and fusing various coloured rods of glass. When the composite rods are sliced, the famous discs of colour remain.

ᛞ Walking Tour

San Pietro Martire

Murano glass chandeliers hang in this brick church, which dates back to 1363. Gravely damaged by fire, it was rebuilt in the Renaissance style then modified over the centuries. Note the Renaissance main door with its large stained-glass window made of *rui*, small circular sections of Murano glass. Inside are **paintings★** by illustrious artists such as Salviati, Veronese, Tintoretto, Bellini and Palma il Giovane.

Seeing Certosa and Murano

Murano sits about 1km/0.6mi to the northeast of Venice and is broken up by several wide canals. To get to Murano, board *vaporetto* line 12, 13, 41 or 42 at Fondamenta Nuove. Once you hop off the *vaporetto*, you can easily see Certosa in an hour. Allow about 2hr 30min.

🏛 Museo del Vetro★

Open year-round Thu–Tue 10am–6pm (Nov–Easter 5pm). Last admission 1hr before closing. Closed 1 Jan, 1 May, 25 Dec. €5.50. 041 73 95 86. www.museicivicivenezian.it.
Palazzo Giustinian explores the evolution of glassmaking over the centuries and is a good place to see quality work before you go off to the shops. An archaeological section displays embalming tools, cups, utensils and necklaces.
On the first floor, the physical processes practised by tradition and modern technology, including coloured glass and *murrine,* are explained with illuminated panels and samples of raw materials. Developments in technique between the 15C and 18C are also defined. The height of artistry attained in the 15C is represented by a wedding cup, traditionally known as the **Barovier Cup**.

Basilica dei SS Maria e Donato★★

Open year-round Mon–Sat 9am– noon & 3.30–7pm, Sun 3.30–7pm. 041 73 90 56.
Be sure to go inside to see the striking **mosaic floor★★**. Look for the two cockerels bearing a fox, which represent the defeat

of Cunning by Vigilance. Children can enjoy finding them, as well as peacocks, eagles and other fanciful creatures. The **apse** is a masterpiece of 12C Veneto-Byzantine art. A double series of blind-arched openings resting on coupled columns ripples around the semicircular bay.
See also the brilliant 12C blue *Virgin in Prayer* set in a gold background. Founded in the 7C, the church was originally dedicated to the Virgin Mary. San Donato's arrival dates from the 12C, when his remains, together with those of the dragon that he had slain, arrived from Cefalonia (the bones of the "dragon" are stored behind the altar). Considerably remodelled in the 12C, the mosaic floor was completed in 1141, and extensively restored during the mid 19C. Inside, five columns with Veneto-Byzantine capitals separate the nave from the aisles.

Isola della Certosa

Settled by monks around 1086 and home to a charterhouse since the 15C, the island eventually fell into disuse and in 1968 was used for storage and later abandoned. This nautical, rustic island is only a 15-minute *vaporetto* ride from San Marco (be sure to request the staff to stop on the way to Murano, as it stops on request only).
Certosa has a small hotel and a good restaurant. To return to San Marco or to go toward Murano, on the dock press the signal button and a light tells the *vaporetto* captain which direction you wish to go in.

BURANO★★

Burano is the most colourful of the lagoon islands. At the doors and windows of the houses, painted in the brightest colours of the rainbow, the occasional lacemaker works on pillows while the men attend to their fishing nets and boats. Visitors may be hailed with friendly "invitations" from the locals selling *passementerie* (articles bordered in lace) displayed by the "lace-houses".

A Bit of History

Venice has been known for lace-making since the 16C. The practice was first established in the palaces as a domestic activity, before it spread to hospitals and women's institutions where residents took up the occupation to secure income. Traditional production depended on the combined use of the needle and bobbin, and proliferated until the second half of the 17C, when demand was threatened by competition from France, which ironically had instituted an industry employing Venetian lacemakers. During the 18C the Venetian authorities were forced to take measures to halt the exodus of lacemakers; certain manufacturers such as **Raniere e Gabrieli** were granted preferential privileges and traditional methods were compromised, allowing for a simpler, bobbin-only technique to be used. Between the 18C and 19C, however, demand dwindled until eventually the production of lace for clothing was discontinued. By the second decade of the 19C there were just two lace factories left, one in Venice and one on Burano, and needlepoint continued as a private, domestic pastime. A school was set up in 1872 to safeguard designs and practices. Lifestyles changed in the 20C and few had the domestic servants or inclination to clean, iron and maintain lace properly. Today very

Colorful façades of Burano

©michel1164/Fotolia.com

Burano lies about 8km/5mi northeast of Venice just south of the island of Torcello. It takes about 45min to get from Fondamenta Nuove (line 12) to Burano, which you can also reach from the Faro (Lighthouse) stop on Murano. The last stretch of the journey is along the Mazzorbo Canal, which separates Burano from the island of Mazzorbo. The two islands are linked by a wooden bridge. Allow a couple of hours to visit the island.

little lace is made in the traditional way as it is so labour-intensive – it is said that it takes three years for ten women to make a single medium-sized tablecloth. It is therefore very expensive and any cheap lace is almost certainly from China.

Piazza Baldassarre Galuppi

The square is dominated by the austere façade of the 16C Church of San Martino and its 18C campanile, built by Andrea Tirali, which leans 1.85m/6ft 1in. Inside is a great sarcophagus around which a miracle is said to have happened. It is explained in a painting, the *Miracle of the Children and the Urn*, attributed to **Alessandro Zanchi**. The inhabitants of Burano also attribute their sparing from the

plague in 1630 to the divine intervention of their patrons. The skeletons of three saints today lie in the altar below the sarcophagus. Off the piazza on via Baldassare Galuppi opposite the Galuppi restaurant is Burano's most **colourful house**.

🏛 Museo del Merletto (Lace Museum)

Open year-round Wed–Mon 10am–5pm (Nov–Easter 4pm). Closed 1 Jan, 1 May, 25 Dec. €4. 041 73 00 34. www.museicivicivenezianii.it.

An important collection of collars, napkins, parasols, bedspreads, centrepieces, handkerchiefs and lace edgings is on display in this recently restored museum. Practical demonstrations by experts.

Museo del Merletto

Mazzorbo

Mazzorbo was – and still is – a sleepy-looking island, linked to Burano by a long footbridge and worth a look. In recent years a winery project began a revival of the grape varietal that grows on the island, and to revitalise its vineyards.

The result – **Venissa** – expanded the vineyards that yielded the golden Dorna wine made by Bisol, to include a small hostel and excellent restaurant. The island also has the excellent old-fashioned family-run Trattoria Maddalena that remains open year-round. It's worth getting off here, as the walk from the Mazzorbo stop to Burano is only about five minutes and you can take a detour through the vineyard, stop for a glass of wine at Venissa, have lunch at Maddalena or dinner at either.

Excursion

San Francesco del Deserto★
041 528 6863.
www.sanfrancescodeldeserto.it.
This little island just south of Burano is ideal for anyone seeking respite from commotion and crowds, particularly in high summer when the islands of the lagoon can get very busy. The island where St Francis landed is still only accessible by private boat today. Take the *vaporetto* (12, 14 or 6) to Burano, then take a water taxi, or negotiate a ride with one of the fishermen. They depart from Burano where the canal meets the lagoon as it laps the water's edge in Piazza Galuppi. The cost includes the 10-minute ferry ride and waiting time; ask the boatman about the price. It is also possible to spend a few

days in retreat with the monastic community by prior arrangement. **Monastery** – *Visit by guided tour only (1hr) Tue–Sun 9am–11am & 3–5pm. Donation requested.*
Before St Francis landed on the island on his way back from the Holy Land in 1220, San Francesco del Deserto was known as the *Isola delle due Vigne* (the Island of the Two Vines). Its name was changed when a house for Franciscan novitiates was established on the island in 1224. The term *"deserto"* could be a reference to the island left "deserted" when the monks fled from a malaria epidemic. On four occasions the monastery played host to Bernardino of Siena, who may have paid for the well to be dug to collect water. Set into a wall in the cloisters is a 13C relief of two crossed arms, said to be that of Christ and St Francis.
Today around seven friars live here, their number augmented by novices who generally stay for a year or so.
The **guided tour** (1hr) is undertaken by a Franciscan monk and takes in various paintings depicting the saint arriving on the island and the miracle of St Francis ordering the birds to be quiet and not to move during prayers. A panel covers some interesting archaeological remains, including a cistern.
The island's beautiful and vast cypress-scented **park**, offering an almost pastoral atmosphere, is possibly the most peaceful place in the whole Venetian archipelago. It overlooks the lagoon and affords a clear view of Burano.

TORCELLO★★

Torcello has drawn the famous and infamous for centuries, from Attila the Hun (452) to Charlie Chaplin, as well as literary figures like Ernest Hemingway and John Ruskin. Ruskin wrote of the relationship between Torcello and Venice in melancholy terms: "Mother and Daughter, you behold them both in their widowhood". As you step onto the landing stage there is a beautiful Mother and Child relief high on the wall above, to contemplate. From here, a walk along the Fondamenta dei Borgognoni, and on by the canal, allows a full prospect of the unique lagoon landscape to unfold. Once more important than Venice, these days Torcello is an atmospheric overgrown near-ghost island, where only the stones speak of its glorious past.

A Bit of History

Near the **Ponte del Diavolo** (the Devil's Bridge) stands the religious complex of Torcello. Alongside are a handful of restaurants and possibly some itinerant lace sellers. It is incredible to think that in ancient times there were around 20 000 people (some estimates go as high as 50 000) living on the island while the glorious history of Venice was only just beginning.

During the period of barbarian invasions, the Lombards chased out the Byzantines (6C–8C) and established themselves in Aquilea, Padua, Altinum and Oderzo. The bishop and the inhabitants of Altinum moved to Torcello where, in 639, the church and probably the fortifications were built; it is the *torri* (towers) of such fortifications that gave rise to the name of the island. They were

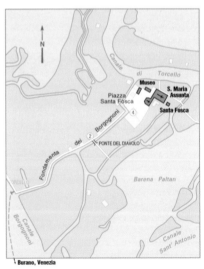

WHERE TO EAT

Al Ponte del Diavolo...②
Locanda Cipriani.........④

TORCELLO

0   200 m
0   200 yds

N

Canale di Torcello

Museo
Piazza Santa Fosca
S. Maria Assunta
④
Santa Fosca

del Borgognoni
② PONTE DEL DIAVOLO

Fondamenta

Barena Paltan

Canale Borgognoni

Canale Sant'Antonio

↘ Burano, Venezia

Seeing Torcello

Torcello lies about 8km/5mi to the northeast of Venice. From Fondamenta Nuove, take the same line (12) that goes to Burano, which is only minutes away from Torcello. Allow a minimum of 2hrs to take in the atmosphere.

not the first inhabitants, however, as the Romans had already discovered the island and records show continuous fishing and glassmaking activities throughout the 5C and 6C. Torcello's decline started around the 10C and mirrors the pace of the glorious ascent of Venice. When malaria infested the marshes, Torcello was abandoned by its inhabitants, who fled to Venice and Murano. Now there are only around 20 inhabitants who live here year-round.

Basilica di Santa Maria Assunta

Open Mar–Oct 10.30am–6pm, Nov–Feb 10am–5pm. Last admission 30min before closing. €4 (€7.50 combined ticket with Museum or Campanile; €10 combined ticket with Museo and Campanile). 041 29 60 630.

See this church for the lovely mosaics and for the lagoon view from its bell tower. An ancient **inscription** tells you the cathedral was erected in 639, during the reign of Heraclius, Emperor of Byzantium. The lagoon's oldest building, it's a splendid example of the Veneto-Byzantine style. The structure is simple, but the decoration is opulent. The Roman sarcophagus near the high altar

contains the relics of St Heliodorus, the first Bishop of Altinum. Most striking are the **ancient mosaics★★** representing the Virgin and Christ.

Campanile

Open as Basilica, closes 30min earlier. €4 (€7.50 combined ticket with the Basilica and Museum). 041 29 60 630.

The 12C bell tower climb is not difficult and the **view★★** over the lagoon more than compensates for the effort.

Santa Fosca

Open daily 10am–4.30pm. 041 73 00 84.

This small 11C–12C church in the form of a Greek cross has an octagonal exterior, encircled by columns capped by Veneto-Byzantine capitals. The solemn interior is covered with a round wooden roof.

Museo di Torcello

Open Mar–Oct Tue–Sun 10.30am–5pm; Nov–Mar, daily except Mon, 10am–4.30pm. Closed public hols and 21 Nov. €4 (€7.50 combined ticket with the Basilica or Campanile; €10 combined ticket with the Basilica and the Campanile). 041 26 90 329. http:// sbmp.provincia.venezia.it.

Historical artefacts from Torcello displayed on two floors. Interesting pieces include capitals, pateras, tablets, a mid-15C wooden *Pietà* of the Venetian School, a work from the studio of Veronese, and books and documents which recount parts of the island's history.

OUTLYING ISLANDS

CHIOGGIA

Chioggia, a lagoon fishing port, shares some architectural similarities with Venice, but the traffic – by foot, by sea and by car – is constant. Chioggia is one of Italy's busiest fishing ports, full of frenetic urgency. Its wooden fishing wharves are exciting to watch.

A Bit of History

Clodia, Chioggia's former name, derives from a channel of the Brenta Delta. In the 1C BC the Romans transformed it into a commercial harbour. Saltpans were the major business in the 11C and 12C, but were devastated between 1378 and 1381, when Chioggia became the field of battle between rivals Genoa and Venice. La Serenissima was victorious, but Chioggia was annihilated. Rebuilding began and continued over the ensuing century. Venice planned to reinforce Chioggia as a lagoon defence. The town grew up close to the sea, centred around Corso del Popolo and the Canale della Vena. From the 16C fishing began to supersede the saltpans as the main industry. In the 19C Chioggia's isolation was in part breached by the building of the bridge carrying the Romea road.

Sights

The main street, the **Corso del Popolo**, runs parallel to the Canale della Vena – the Fossa Clodia of Ancient times – colourful and lively at its excellent **fish market** (open every morning except Monday) and ending at Piazzetta Vigo. The column bearing a winged lion marks the end of the Fossa Clodia. To cross the canal, walk over the stone bridge, the Ponte Vigo, built in 1685. The *corso* is dotted with the Duomo and several of the Chioggia churches, among them the Church of **San Andrea**, with its 11C Romanesque *campanile* rising from a square base. **San Giacomo** was rebuilt in the 18C; **San Francesco delle Muneghette** was founded in the 15C but rebuilt 18C. At the far end of Chioggia, the **Isola di San Domenico** is reached by following Calle di San Croce, beyond Ponte Vigo.

At the other end of the island to the bus stop are two small museums; the **Museo Diocesano d'Arte Sacra**, Sacred Art Museum (*041 55 07 477, www.chioggiatourism.it*) and close by the **Museo della Laguna Sud** (*041 55 00 911, www.chioggiatourism.it/eng*).

Seeing Chioggia

Strictly speaking, Chioggia is not one of the lagoon islands, as it rests on two parallel islands, linked to terra firma by a long bridge. It lies about 19km/12mi south of Venice (as the crow flies), along the Adriatic Sea, and just north of the Brenta Valley. Visitors touring the neighbouring area, perhaps after a visit to the Brenta villas, will find it easy to approach Chioggia on the SS 309, which has beautiful views over the Venetian Lagoon. Alternatively, a coach service operates every 30min from Piazzale Roma to Chioggia-Sottomarina taking around 1hr. Don't miss the fish market. For a leisurely walk around Chioggia allow a couple of hours.

SAN LAZZARO DEGLI ARMENI ★

Romantic poet Lord Byron loved this island, as he found the atmosphere lifted his ascetic spirit in times of melancholy. Today, it is no less evocative to visitors. On arrival by *vaporetto*, tourists are greeted by charming Armenian monks who chaperone their charges and introduce them to this green, serene island.

Armenians and the Mechitar Community

The Armenians link their ancestry to Noah's Ark, which some believe "ran aground" on Mount Ararat, on the Armenian border. Armenia then extended from the Black Sea to Mesopotamia, where the mountains hide the sources of the River Tigris and River Euphrates. Today the Republic of Armenia is hemmed in between Turkey, Georgia, Azerbaijan and Iran. The country was conquered on several occasions by the Arabs, Turks, Mongols, Tartars, Ottomans and Persians. During the First World War, its people were persecuted by the Turks, almost to the point of extinction. Subsequent diaspora saw the Armenians flee overseas. From the 14C, the island of San Lazzaro served as a leper colony until the last two leprosy sufferers were transferred to Venice (1600s). The Venetian Republic gave the island to the **Mechitar**, who arrived here in 1717.

The church was rebuilt, the pavement lifted, the arches made into lancet arches and the vaulted ceiling took the form of a starry sky. The original Romanesque church was remodelled in the Gothic style.

Visit

Visit by guided tours only (1hr 15min), daily 3–5pm. €6. 041 52 60 104.

In total there are 10 monks plus 10 seminarians, and around 15 Armenian students who study Italian language and culture. Visitors are shown the refectory where the monks and the seminarists eat their meals in silence while the Scriptures are read out in classical Armenian. The monastery also has a collection of Flemish tapestries, paintings by Armenian artists, Greek, Phoenician and Assyro-Babylonian artefacts and an archive of Armenian volumes and manuscripts dating back some 1300 years.

Seeing San Lazzaro degli Armeni

The island is located near the Lido, off the west side. It takes about 30min to get to the island of San Lazzaro degli Armeni on *vaporetto* line 20 from Riva degli Schiavoni (San Zaccaria). Tours are scheduled to coincide with the *vaporetto* times – the talk begins on landing and continues through the monastery visit. Should you require more time on the island, catch the *vaporetto* that leaves at around 2pm and check for the departure time of the second return service. The tour takes about 1hr 15mins.

GONDOLAS

The sleek black gondola has evolved over 1,000 years. For centuries its form and beauty have captured the attention of artists and visitors alike. Made of seven different types of wood, its hull is black by tradition and 17C law. A gondola takes over a month to build and there are only three *squeri*, gondola boatyards, left in Venice. Gondolas once numbered in the thousands, but now there are only about 350.

Gondolas

No one knows exactly when the gondola was invented: the word *gundula* appears as early as 1094 in a decree of Doge Vitale Falier, although the reference relates to a massive boat equipped with a large crew of rowers – a far cry from the gondola we know today.

In the 14C small boats covered with a central canopy bore metal decorations on the prow and stern. At the end of the century the vessel began to be made longer and lighter, the prow and stern were raised and the **felze** or cabin was added, affording shelter in bad weather. Some had decorated prows, others were painted in bright colours and decked with satin, silk and gleaming brass. On the prow and stern stood painted cherubs bearing the coat of arms of the family to which the gondola belonged. From the 16C, boats were toned down by being painted black: a colour we might judge to be funereal, but in Venice red, not black, is the colour of mourning. Today the gondola is about 11m/36ft long, 1.42m/4ft wide and comprises 280 pieces of wood.

Tips for Visitors

If you specify your own route or request a singing gondolier, the rate should be negotiated in advance with the gondolier. Enquire, too, about extras like champagne, ice bucket and glasses. Keep in mind that air temperature over the water may be cooler, so you might want to have a wrap. If you don't have the budget, take

Gondolas

©Gwen Cannon/Michelin

one of the gondola ferries, or *traghetti,* across the Grand Canal, where the fare is only €0.50. *See Planning Your Trip for full costs.*

Building a Gondola

The shipyards where gondolas are built and repaired are called **squeri**. At one time, each of these was allocated primarily to a family from Cadore in the Dolomites, which explains why their wooden galleried constructions resembled alpine houses. The **ferro**, a sabre-toothed projection made of iron placed at the prow and stern, is the most crucial element of the gondola: implemented initially as a fender to safeguard against knocks, today it serves as a counterweight to the gondolier, and is used to align the boat around hazards in the narrowest passages. The curved fin is said to echo the doge's *corno* (cap) and to symbolise its power over the six **sestieri** or divisions of the city represented by the six serrations. The tooth that "guards" the gondola itself is the Giudecca. The **forcola**, or rowlock, is an intricate piece of carving hewn from walnut, designed as a pivot that allows the oar maximum mobility. The oar is made of well-seasoned beech. But perhaps only the most observant will notice the two bronze sea horses cleating the cords of the seats.

Paline, Dame and Bricole

Whether travelling by gondola, *vaporetto* or other boat, there is always the risk of running aground. Navigable channels are identified by means of **bricole** – a series of large poles (*pali*) roped together – whereas the entrance to a canal or a junction is indicated by **dame**, which are smaller poles than the *bricole*. The **paline** are the thin individual poles that project from the water at odd intervals, to which private craft are tethered. They are particularly evocative if painted with coloured swirling stripes, outside some fine building to mark the landing stage of a patrician family in days gone by.

The Bridges

Among the hundreds of Venetian bridges crossed during the tussles of *su e zo per i ponti*, meaning "up and down the bridges", there are several like the Ponte Chiodo (*see Ca' D'oro*) without railings or parapet, where rival factions such as the Castellani and Nicolotti faced each other during "fist fights" (*see I Carmini*). Projects for bridges with three Arches Met With Less Success (*See Il Ghetto*).

© H. Leue/Look/Photononstop

Gondola and Bridge of Sighs

CARNIVAL

The best way to enjoy 🎭 Carnevale is to jump into the action and get dressed up yourself. The city has no lack of costumes to rent or masks to buy, but it's best to book early. Or arrive with your own. Hotels book up months in advance. Venetians either leave town or celebrate in private parties and balls. *For a full list of events and festivals in Venice, see Planning Your Trip.*

History

During the 18C, the Venice Carnival opened at the beginning of October and ended on the Tuesday preceding Lent, with only one short interruption for Christmas festivities. In those days, masks were worn throughout the Carnival but they were also used in other circumstances: during the Fiera della Sensa lasting for two weeks, on the occasion of doges' elections and their sons' weddings, and when famous personalities arrived in town.

Today, the Carnival starts 10 days before Lent (Feb–Mar) with the "volo dell'angelo" or "flight of the angel". In this ceremony, an acrobat descends the belltower of St Mark's and glides over the piazza to the Doges' Palace by means of two ropes. In the past, the acrobat was dressed as a Turk rather than an angel.

"Buongiorno, siora mascara"

For information on where to buy Carnival costumes and masks, see Shopping.

A key feature of Carnival is the mask. Tradition holds that masks were first introduced to Venice in 1204 when Doge Enrico Dandolo brought veiled Muslim women back to Venice after his conquest of Constantinople. As in Mozart's opera *Don Giovanni* (Act 2), during the 17C masked people greeted each other routinely with the saying "Buongiorno Siora Mascara". To go about one's business dressed in the *baùta* – a mask complete with its hooded black shawl – was so normal that a formal request was lodged by the clergy for Venetians to remove their disguise at least in church.

Return of the Carnival

The greater the decline of Venice, the sharper her sense of fun. Come 1797 when the French assumed power, thus ending the glory of the Venetian Republic for all time, the city continued her revelries, thriving on her taste for jokes and riddles, laughter and carnival, which was eventually revived late in the 19C.

Carnevale di Venezia, Piazza San Marco

©Venezia Marketing ed Eventi

Costumed for Carnival

©R. Mattes/MICHELIN

Even when this modern carnival was reinstated, with an open invitation to all to congregate in Piazza San Marco – the only time the space is truly filled by the crowds – it was a masked attendance. Whether it be with the *baùta*, the full-length cloak (*tabarro*), the three-horned hat (*tricorno*) or the long-nosed mask (*maschera a becco*) that doctors used to wear during the plague epidemics, the rule of the game is always the same: never investigate the identity of the person wearing the mask.

The need to don a mask seems to come as second nature to a Venetian. Maybe because, in the words of Silvio Ceccat:

"The streets are narrow, the population is small. You meet someone at every corner. Everyone knows everyone else's business. Today there are no cars to protect anonymity as yesterday there were no coaches in which to hide … People used to and still do feel naked in Venice. So naked, indeed, that clothes are not enough and hence the need for the mask …".

Masks also serve as a leveller of social class, although dress, shoes and wigs would reveal much.

Today's festivities are organised by the city and include various colourful historic pageants and performances.

The finale is the Grand Ball in the Piazza on Shrove Tuesday. As only A-list celebrities and the great and good of Venice are allowed to attend this jamboree, mere mortals have to content themselves with lesser private and public parties. There is also a huge fireworks display.

Tips for Visitors

When seeking a mask, look for a traditional one made of papier-mâché by a local artisan.

You might like to choose a mask to hang on the wall, as a reminder of your Venice journey. At the peak of Carnevale, pick an area where you would like to celebrate and plan your cocktails, meals, balls, and parties at close range.

The streets will be so congested that you won't be able to move from place to place. If you expect to use transportation, book taxis or gondolas in advance.

Layered costumes are useful if you plan to spend most of the night outside.

CARNIVAL

103

ARTS FESTIVALS

The sensualty and beauty of Venice, its rich cultural heritage, and sense of fun would seem a match with arts festivals like a gondola to water. The two festivals that claim the most international attention are the Venice Film Festival and the Biennale, with plenty of talent, business deals, spectators, celebrations and cocktail posing. Other Biennale events include Festival Internazionale di Musica Contemporanea and the newer addition, in even years, Architecture Biennale.

🎬 Venice Film Festival

The Venice Film Festival unfolds late August or early September and is Venice's most glamorous bash, without the masks.

Stars are born or implode, careers and hits are launched, and flops are well dissected. Action centres at the **Lido**, but related events and parties (and celebrity sitings) will pop up around Venice. Outdoor film screenings are held in **Campo San Polo** after their previews on the Lido. This is high season: best rooms (and yachts) are booked months ahead (even more elusive in odd years when the Biennale is on). For tickets to screenings, check the festival website.

🎬 La Biennale

The world's most prestigious art festival runs June–November and gets under way every odd-numbered year, next in 2013 and 2015.

The 100-year-plus history of this international exhibition of contemporary art (Esposizione Internazionale d'Arte della Citta di Venezia) is long and controversial. Even at its beginnings in 1895, it caused an outcry by exhibiting a painting called *Il Supremo Convegno* by **Giacomo Grosso**.

It was described as "A casket with a cadaveric face coming out, while five naked young women surrounded him in despairing and lusty posing". Over a century later, at almost every Biennale, the same charges have been levelled. Often the Biennale is said to thrive on conflict and controversy; its position in the eye of the storm ensures a restlessness that guarantees its vitality. No doubt it would be deemed a failure if it had not insulted or outraged a particular party for that year!

Pavilions set in the **Arsenale** are the centre of action, but the whole city seems decked out with exhibits in *palazzi* and public spaces. Art enthusiasts plan a few days of full immersion, while other visitors are content to explore for a few hours. Look for well-established artists as well as emerging talent.

Venetian Events

For a full list of events and festivals in Venice, see Planning Your Trip. All events are listed under www.labiennale.org.

BEACHES

Whether or not you are a beach enthusiast, everyone should come to the Lido's east shore to see the Adriatic Sea. Only then does the full picture of Venice, once a great sea power and still very much connected with the sea, begin to emerge.

Lido

Beaches June–Sept 9.30am–6pm.

The Romantic poets, including Byron, made a splash at the Lido beaches, where the first beach platforms went up in 1857. In 1888, the first wooden *capanne* were erected, a handy place where the family could change, play and lunch. Posh turn-of-the-20C hotels like **Des Bain** and **Excelsior** launched the Lido as one of the world's first luxury beach resorts. If you prefer a casual, economical approach, try the south end of the Lido, good for nature lovers who prefer to avoid the social scene. Swimmers will appreciate that the water quality received Bandiera Blu (Blue Flag) awards for its cleanliness in 2009, and, toward the south end, in 2011. The glamorous **stabilmenti** *(beach facilities; most stabilmenti open in June and close early September, when transport is more frequent, too; hours, unless otherwise noted, are usually 8.30am–7pm)* are protective of their turf, for which affluent sun-worshippers pay upwards of €15,000 for the season for their privacy, so expect daily rates for a *lettino* (lounge chair) and *ombrellone* (umbrella) at Excelsior or Des Bains to have posh price tags, too. Day-trippers are quickly shooed away, although in 2011 Venice's mayor caused controversy with the glitterati by declaring that all have the right to swim within 5m/15ft of the shoreline, whether private or public.

Getting Around

Getting around on the Lido by land is relatively easy. From the **vaporetto** stop on the west, to the east shore beaches is a short walk. To go up and down the island, **buses** run from the *vaporetto* stop. Cycling is the most fun, though. In

Lido beach

©Videocomunicazione Città di Venezia

BEACHES

105

2011 Venice began a 🚲 **bicycle sharing** programme: using a **tessera** (prepaid card), you unlatch the bike from designated points at **Piazzale S. Maria Elisabetta** or **Via Candia** (Palazzo del Cinema); ride around, then park it at either location when you return. This began as an experiment during the 2011 Film Festival with 10 bikes/15 parking spots (a similar system is in place in Mestre). You can purchase an annual pass from Uffici ASM (*via Pisani 10, Lido*, €15). The first hour is free, the second hour is €1, and each hour after is €2. For half-day or all-day use, enquire about rentals from a bike shop or your hotel.

You can also navigate the lagoon on a 🚲 **bragozzo** (*388 182 6009/6010, www.ilbragozzo.it*), and book a half or full-day excursion on the traditional lagoon boat.

The Lido is well served by transport, even at night, so keep the Lido in mind off season for bargain accommodation, although many hotels close.

Alas, after closing down for a few years, the luxurious Thomas Mann *Death in Venice* hotel has been converted to 🚲 **Residence Des Bains** and now a stay there will require locating an apartment more likely by the week, season, or year; although for a hefty sum you can wallow in luxury for the day.

Excelsior / Amaranti Beach

Excelsior Spiagge, Lungomare Marconi, Lido di Venezia, 041 271 6836.

Refined beach huts adorned with white curtains in front of the Hotel Excelsior mark off movie-star territory. The only shouting here should be a director yelling "cut!" Exclusive with prices to match.

Des Bains Beach

Lungomare Marconi, Lido di Venezia, 041 271 6808.

Residence (formerly Hotel) Des Bains is early 20C nostalgia. Described by Thomas Mann in *Death in Venice*, the quaint thatched roofs are the only rustic touch, where elegance is top of the agenda, as are prices.

Quattro Fontane Beach

041 271 6862.

Exclusive atmosphere, but emphasises its "young, dynamic, vivacious atmosphere" for bathing beauties. Expensive.

Bagni Alberoni

On the southern tip of the Lido, near a WWF wildlife reserve. Strada Nuova dei Bagni 26, Alberoni, Lido di Venezia, 041 731 029.

The owner prides himself on maintaining a wholesome family atmosphere at reasonable prices with beach facilities (€16 for *lettino* and *ombrellone*) and a kid-pleasing restaurant with pizza and other fare. This beach received the Bandiera Blu award in 2011.

🚲 WWF Alberoni

Operated by World Wildlife Fund (www.wwf.it), Alberoni, Lido di Venezia, 041 971 384.

Not for beach bums, this is a naturalistic observatory for nature-lovers who want to see the plantlife and wildlife of the lagoon; the best seasons are spring and autumn. You can book a guide, too.

MUST DO

FOR KIDS

Venice's extraordinary surroundings will be as fascinating for children as they are for older visitors. Venice has few specific attractions aimed at children, but with a little imagination, you can design outings that adults, too, will cherish. Treat them to a gondola ride. Climb bell towers to enjoy the wonderful view of the city and the lagoon. Any time of year, plan a visit to the sea. In summer swim at one of the Lido beaches. Year-round bike along the coast. Watch fishermen and see their catch on the islands of Pellestrina or Chioggia.

Gondolas

Older kids will love a leisurely **gondola ride** (see p100) or the economical short gondola ride on a **traghetto** (see p17). Gondola **boatyards** (see p50, 56) also offer interesting glimpses of real life.

Vaporetto Journeys

Vaporetto journeys are sure to be a hit. Best to buy an ACTV transport pass for the maximum number of days that you are in Venice; individual rides become expensive. As well as taking in the views of Venice from the sea, the *vaporetto* takes you to the outlying islands where you can swim, run, climb, sail, picnic, and watch glassblowing. If you are lucky enough to find seats, the *vaporetto* also makes a good break from walking.

Boating About

Take a sailing lesson, hire a kayak, or book a sailboat excursion on **Certosa** (see p92). The **Zattere** (see p49) also offers a non-stop spectacle of boats of all shapes and sizes. Have lunch or dinner at La Piscina, with delicious food at reasonable prices, or stop for a drink or their home-made ice cream (better than the *gelaterie* nearby). Historically this spot was popular with kids, where until only a few decades ago, they swam in the

piscina (swimming pool), a little area of the canal that was roped off.

Lido

Take the *vaporetto* to the **Lido**, then walk to the east coast and the Adriatic Sea. Spend an afternoon at the beach, hike, or bike. At Nicelli Airport (San Nicolò district), you can book a helicopter flight (*www.heliairvenice.com*) over the lagoon, or nearby watch smaller planes take off and land over the lagoon. Gaze at the heavens in the free planetarium, Planetario di Venezia Lido (*www.museicivicineziani.it*).

Picnics

The previous mayor launched a campaign to bring back decorum to Venice. Unless at a café, eating in public squares is out, likewise on canals or church steps. Find the ingredients at a good food shop, then hop on the *vaporetto* for **Certosa**, **Torcello** or the **Lido**. Certosa has plenty of grassy areas and ruins from the former convent that make for a tranquil setting, while the Lido has some free beaches. All have plenty of room to run and places to kick a ball.

Glassblowing

In the morning, take the *vaporetto* to the **Murano** Faro (Lighthouse) stop; hop off and wander around the glass factories. Some will try to lure you in for a free glassblowing demonstration. Enjoy it, but be prepared for the sales pitch afterwards. An authentic souvenir made in Murano will cost more than the foreign imitations that are widely sold, but try to select glass that was made here, even if it's only a pendant, button, or key-ring. Take *vaporetto* 42 which circles through Murano (stops at Colonna, Faro, Museo and others); near the Serenella stop, look for boatbuilder **Cantiere Serenella**, where they might be working on motorboats in the shipyard or have one up on a crane.

Secret Passages

Follow secret passages and routes through the **Doges' Palace**. English-language tours, €18, depart at 9.55am, 10.45am and 11.45am. Book at least five days ahead or go to the ticket office (*www. museicivicivenezani.it*).

Bell-tower Climbing

Burn off some energy right in busy San Marco; the **campanile** (see p32) and the **Torre dell'Orologio** (see p36) are two towers to climb. Ride the vaporetto to climb **San Giorgio Maggiore** (see p85) and for a good view of San Marco and the lagoon. Take a relaxing longer ride south in the lagoon to the rather wild island of **Torcello** to climb **Santa Maria Assunta**'s bell tower (see p97), then see the animal mosaics.

Art Treasure Hunt

Begin in the undervisited **Archaeological Museum** (see p36), right on Piazza San Marco. Look at some of the most famous sculptures, then, as you visit museums and churches, see if you can identify any of the sculptures in the paintings. Or try this with city palaces, seascapes and landscapes: find your favourite palazzo, or look for mountain backgrounds just like those you see on a clear day from Certosa or the vaporetto toward Burano.

Natural History

See the creatures of the Venice lagoon in the **Natural History Museum** (see p73), then hop on a vaporetto and hike around the nature observatory on the **Lido** (see p89), or take a walk around **Certosa** (see p92) or **Torcello** (see p96) to see whether you see any birds or animals that were in the museum and what types of habitats you can identify.

Casa di Corto Maltese

Meet the characters of **Corto Maltese** (www.lacasadicorto.it) and design some of your own.

Student Art Exhibits

Watch for art shows at local schools or at **Ca' Foscari** (see p22, 82), where university fine arts students periodically open their studios to the public.
You'll probably only find out about these by posters that may be in local bars, on billboards or near schools.

Costumes

Dress up in **masks** and **costumes** and wander Venice in the century of your choice or as your favourite character. No need to wait for Carnival, this is Venice! Masks or costumes are ok here any hour, day or night.

ENTERTAINMENT

The play of evening lights on the lamplit canals and floodlit *palazzi* is a memorable sight, especially from the vantage point of a slow gliding gondola. Evening entertainment is low-key, though widespread in summer, in the theatres, churches, bars and cafés. Since the time of Goldoni and Pietro Longhi, Venice has been the perfect backdrop for theatre. Festivals and drama are still very much a part of life.

What's On?

The **tourist office** has a free calendar of Shows and Events on a monthly basis (see p13): evening performances are listed day by day. The office also offers a free, event-packed booklet entitled Un Ospite di Venezia: see the Venice by Night section. Information is also available online at *www.unospitedivenezia.it and www.turismovenezia.it* (click on Events); both sites are also in English.

At the weekend the magazine of the daily newspaper, **Il Gazettino**, provides comprehensive coverage of the shows, exhibitions and festivals held in Venice, as well as concerts and recitals in churches and public buildings.

Information on theatre, cinema and concerts in Venice is also available at *www.culturaspettacolovenezia.it*. Simplest of all, large posters announcing events are plastered throughout the streets, so keep your eyes peeled.

Churches and Scuoli

Also see Districts on following pages.
A Vivaldi concert in one of the city's historic churches is a highlight of any visit. Get the tourist office's Shows and Events calendar and watch the street posters. Churches holding performances usually have a printed announcement at the entrance steps a few days in advance of the event.

Many of the scuoli, such as **Grande di San Teodoro**, **San Giovanni Evangelista** (see p74) and **San Rocco** (see p72), offer evening performances of classical music, often in masks and period costumes. Be prepared to pay in cash, as credit cards are generally not accepted. Plan to arrive early to get good seats and to admire the art.

Courtesy la Biennale di Venezia – ASAC

International Film Festival

Street Music

One of the delights of Venice is the variety of live classical music heard on so many streets and church entrance steps, both day and night.

Cinema

The most important film event in Venice runs from late August to September, when the **International Film Festival** is held at the Lido. After they've previewed, some films screen at the open-air giant screen erected in Campo S. Polo. Book your ticket during the day for showings the same evening.

Hotel Bars

Indulge in the ambience of the city's great hotels without the high cost of a room by having a drink at the **Hotel Bauer** (see p110, 121, 141), Bar Dandolo in **Hotel Danieli** or Bar Longhi in the **Gritti Palace** (see p149). Enjoy your cocktail in the bar or on the outdoor terrace, offering stunning night-time views with royal service.

Hotel Metropole is better known for **Met Restaurant** (*see p147; Riva degli Schiavoni; 4149, 041 524 0344*) than its bar, but the lounge has a wonderfully sumptuous exotic Eastern influence in its comfy décor; its piano bar is open until fairly late, while at a side door canal water laps up the steps.

Districts

San Marco Area

Caffè Quadri A2– *Piazza S. Marco 10*. Additional charge for music. A legendary Venetian haunt, both inside with the period décor or outside on the piazza where the orchestra plays and the smart set come to see and be seen.

Caffè Florian A2– *Piazza S. Marco 56. www.caffeflorian.it. Additional charge for music*. With its marble tables, velvet banquettes, mirrors, gilding and paintings under glass with gilt-wood frames, you have to experience the interior of this historic 1720 café steeped in Venetian legend.

Harry's Bar A2 – *Calle Vallaresso, S. Marco 1323. www.harrysbarvenezia.com. 041 528 5777*. Another institution: this was Hemingway's base during his Venetian sojourns. Famous for its cocktails, try the writer's beloved Montgomery or the Bellini.

Monaco e Gran Canal A2 – *Calle Vallaresso, S. Marco 1332. www.hotelmonaco.it*. Superb view of La Salute and the Grand Canal from the café terrace at the foot of the famous *palazzo*.

Birreria Forst B2 – *Calle delle Rasse, Castello 4540*. A bar focused on beer that also offers *tramezzini* on black bread and cured meats.

Le Bistrot de Venise – *See restaurant listing p130*. This restaurant has an inviting wine bar, with some 500 wines by the glass, plus frequent events including readings, tastings with winemakers, and exhibits that lure Venetians as well as tourists.

Bacaro Lounge Bar – *Salizzada San Moisè, San Marco 1345. 041 296 0687*. This fashionable spot, just off Piazza San Marco, boasts a buzzing red-mosaic-tiled cocktail bar, a glass staircase lined with bottles of wine, and is one of Venice's few spots to dine after midnight.

Birreria Forst – *Calle delle Rasse, 4540. 041 523 0557. Closed Sat in winter*. A typical brasserie where gondoliers meet, with a range of beers and a good selection of snacks, including German-style black-bread würstel sandwiches.

Centrale – *Piscina Frezzeria, San Marco. 041 296 0664. www.centrale-lounge.com. Closed Tue*. Near St Mark's Square in 16C *palazzo* with atmospheric candles and soft lighting, designer armchairs and sofas, ambient chill-out music, DJs and live bands. There is a restaurant serving innovative Mediterranean cuisine, while cocktails and *cichèti* are served until 2am in the lounge bar.

Luna Hotel Baglioni – *Calle Valleresso, San Marco 1243. 041 528 9840*. Early guests here included the Knights Templar, but these days the historic hotel offers occasional classical music dinner concerts, where guests can come for both or just for dinner or the concert, which also attracts locals.

Martini Scala Club – *Calle del Cafétier, 1007 San Marco. 041 522 4121. Closed Tue*. Elegant piano bar with a restaurant, the music starts at around 10pm.

Ai Rusteghi Corte del Tintor – *San Marco 5513 (near S. Bartolomeo Calle de la Bissa and Sottoportego). 041 523 2205. 10.30am–3pm, 6–11pm, closed Sun*. This busy, atmospheric small wine bar next to its own secluded courtyard has a great buzz. Giovanni's selection of wines (over 300 by the glass) is so good that he attracts local restaurateurs and wine merchants who want to see what's in, as well as international visitors. The food options are more ample at lunch, but in between popping corks he manages to proffer some interesting snacks in the evening.

Story of Venice – *Teatro San Gallo, 50m/yd from Piazza San Marco. 041 241 1943. www.venice-carnival-show.com*. Anthony Wilkinson, award-winning writer/director, brings Venice history to life with this exciting show combining live and recorded performances with digital projection and surround-sound technology. All other productions throughout the city are in Italian only, but this should not diminish your enjoyment of dance, opera and concerts.

Rialto Area

Little **wine bars** between the Rialto and the fish market transform *campi* into *aperitivi* gatherings with lively banter.

Bacaro Jazz – *Campo S. Bartolomeo. 041 285 249. www.bacarojazz.com*. Jazz is the theme at this lively cocktail bar and restaurant, near the Rialto Bridge, which also serves snacks, *cichèti* and Sunday brunch.

Devil's Forest – *Calle degli Stagneri 5185. 041 520 0623. www.devilsforest.com. Closed Mon*. A pleasant brasserie for a glass of beer and a game of darts, chess or backgammon.

L'Olandese volante – *Campo S. Lio 5658. 041 528 9349. Closed Sun*. Situated between Campo S. Maria Formosa and Rialto, the Flying Dutchman is known for its good beer and wide choice of salads and snacks.

Teatro Malibran – *Behind the church of San Giovanni Crisostomo. 041 78 66 01. www.teatrolafenice.it*. Plays, operas and classical concerts.

Teatro Goldoni – *Calle del Teatro. 041 24 02 011. www.teatro stabileveneto.it*. Plays and occasional concerts.

La Fenice

🎵 **Gran Teatro La Fenice** – *Campo San Fantin, San Marco. 041 78 65 11. www.teatrolafenice.it.* The city's beloved opera house also hosts ballet and jazz concerts.

The **Interpreti Veneziani** perform regularly at the church of S. Vidal, as well as at the Scuola Grande S. Todaro.

Fondazione Ugo e Olga Levi – *www.fondazionelevi.it.* The foundation, which undertakes extensive research and archival work in the Palazzo Giustinian Lolin, just by the Ponte dell' Accademia, regularly organises concerts.

Musica a Palazzo – *www.musicapalazzo.com.* The Palazzo Barbarigo-Minotto, beside the Grand Canal (access via Campo S. Maria Zobenigo), hosts themed musical evenings: love duets (*La Traviata, Tosca, La Bohème*, Wed and Sat); arias and Neapolitan songs (Mon and Fri) and *La Traviata* (Tue, Thu and Sun). Each act is performed in a different room.

Schiavoni and Arsenale

🎵 **Church of la Pietà** A3 – *Riva degli Schiavoni.* Vivaldi's presence is almost tangible here. Concerts are regularly held to take advantage of the exceptional acoustics.

Ca d'Oro Area

Il Santo Bevitore B3 – *Calle Zancani/ Fond. Diedo - Cannaregio 2420.* Students and regulars drink a beer, watch football on TV and grab a sandwich or the dish of the day.

Al Paradiso Perduto – *Fondamenta de la Misericordia 2540, Cannaregio. 041 720 581. Closed Tue–Wed.* Food and live music in this traditional *osteria*;

one of Venice's favourite late-night spots for many years now.

Sant'Elena and San Pietro

Football fans can watch the local team play at the Stadio P. L. Penzo on the corner of the Fondamenta S. Elena and Viale S. Elena (nearest *vaporetto* stop: S. Elena). Experimental and rare music concerts are some of the programmes of the **Giorgio Cini Foundation** (*www.cini.it*).

Cannaregio and Il Ghetto

Teatro Fondamenta Nuove – *Fondamenta Nuove, Cannaregio. 041 522 44 98. www.teatrofondamentanuove.it.* Programme includes jazz, contemporary music and dance.

🎵 **Casino di Venezia** – *Cannaregio 2040.* Whether or not you plan to try your luck at roulette, if you want an elegant spot for drinks until 2.30am, it's been well tested since 1638. Elegant attire, jackets required.

Dogado – *Via Cannaregio 3660A. 041 520 8544.* A multi-purpose eating and drinking venue, Dogado serves excellent-value food by day in a smart café downstairs, while above, by night, is a smart wine bar, a full à la carte restaurant and roof-top terrace.

The Fiddler's Elbow – *Campo già Testori 3847, Cannaregio. 041 52 39 930. www.thefiddlerselbow.com.* Between the churches of Santa Sofia and San Felice, this Irish pub is a popular place for its beer garden, Irish coffee and sports TV.

SHOPPING

Shopping in Venice is a treat. Venetians have been expert traders, merchants and artisans for centuries, during which the city has been known for its quality, not for its bargains. There are many boutique shops showcasing glass, textiles, fashion, lace, masks, marbelised paper, book bindings and other local products. In some of the shops you can watch artisans at work, such as the glassmakers on the island of Murano. However, there is a proliferation of shops with inexpensive Asian imports. If you are unfamiliar with some of the crafts, seek them out first in museums or quality stores, where you can learn what makes Venetian work special and how to sort it out from imitations.

Business Hours

Most shops are open Mon–Sat, 8am–1pm and 3.30–7.30pm. Credit cards are accepted in most stores. Venice has few department stores. One is **Coin** (San Giovanni Crisostomo in Cannaregio, just north of the Rialto Bridge), carrying affordable fashions, cosmetics and housewares.

Shopping Tips

Crowded narrow streets provide ideal circumstances for pickpockets, so do secure your purse and wallets. If you find something you truly like, you might wish to purchase it on the spot. Most Italian shops do not stock a lot of inventory. Venice presents the additional challenge of being a city in which the first-time visitor is easily lost or may simply expend a great deal of time negotiating crowded streets to return to the store with the desired object. The concept of returning goods is not widely accepted in Italy, where even with complete documentation you might not be given a refund; or perhaps the shop will grant its value in exchange, but you might not find a second item in the same shop that interests you. Expect prices to be high when you pay for quality, but also enjoy finding items that are very high in quality. Many places accept

Murano glass lamps

credit cards, but you might enquire whether discounts are offered for cash payments.

Major Shopping Streets

Calle Larga 22 Marzo – *West of Piazza San Marco*. Designer boutiques, glitzy shops, including shoes and handbags.

Mercerie – *Between Pizza San Marco and the Rialto Bridge*. Upscale boutiques selling leather goods, luggage, clothing, housewares and other merchandise.

Rio Terà Lista di Spagna – *Just east of the train station.* Here you'll find a wide variety of glass, clothing and souvenir shops.

Strada Nuova – *Near Ca' d'Oro in the Cannaregio district*. Bakeries and restaurants intermingle with souvenir stalls, gift shops, food and clothing stores.

In addition there are pricey gift and clothing shops along the **Procuratie Nuovo** bordering Piazza San Marco and heavyweight designer boutiques along **Calle Vallaresso**, just west of the Piazza, leading to Harry's Bar.

What to Buy

Carnival costumes and mask

Venice is a city that delights in a rich tradition of disguise and masked balls, making it the ideal place to look at **costumes**. If authenticity is what you seek, expect high prices, often well over €1,000 when precious textiles and trim are used, plus the hours in construction that require skilled handiwork. Fortunately, most costume shops are also in the rental business, so you can wear a stunning ensemble for a night and

return it the next day. The most sought-after costumes are the elaborate 17C and 18C creations, but some have a good mix from medieval to 19C. You can also bring your own designs and have them custom-made, sometimes in surprisingly rapid time, thanks to skilled seamstresses and plenty of practice.

Masks can be either partial or full, the latter traditionally being made of papier-mâché or even leather. Look at the better mask shops or find one where an artisan is working. Many buyers purchase masks without intending to wear them, but to display them as they would a work of art. You might like the mask not only for its design, but also for the character that it represents in associated plays and stories.

To hire a typical Venetian Carnival costume contact **Il Prato**, *Frezzeria 1771, San Marco, 041 520 33 75*; **Nicoloa Atelier**, *Cannaregio 5565, 041 520 70 51*; or **Falpalà**, *Frezzeria 1826, San Marco, 041 52 25 022*. Venetian masks are sold on virtually every street corner; if you are looking for a good-quality mask, opt for one made of papier-mâché by an artisan. Reputable shops include **Ca' Macana**, *Dorsoduro 3172, 041 27 76 142, www.camacana.com;* **La pietra filosofale**, *San Marco 1735 (Frezzeria, not far from the Fenice Theatre);* and **Tragicomica**, *San Polo 2800 (Calle dei Nomboli, near Campo San Tomà), open 7 days, 041 72 11 02, www.tragicomica.it*. **Sergio and Massimo Boldrin** made masks for Stanley Kubrick's *Eyes Wide Shut*; their shop **La Botega dei Mascareri** is by the Rialto (*San Polo 80, 041 524*

2887). In Castello, for masks and costumes try Atelier Marega on *Fodamento dell'Osmarin 4968*. And at **Mondonovo Maschere**, *Dorsoduro 3063 (Rio Terà Canal, near Campo Santa Margherita, 041 52 87 344)*, you can watch master craftsman Guerrino Lovato at work perhaps on a creation for La Fenice.

Glass

Venetian glass is famous worldwide. In lighting, a Venetian glass chandelier is perhaps the ultimate status symbol. There are many other glass objects to enjoy, from sculpture to vases, goblets, earrings, necklaces or beads. Watch glassblowing in Murano to see what skills are required and which special techniques are used to achieve particular effects.

The most famous glass store in the city is **Venini** (*Piazzetta dei Leoni*), a longtime tenant of Piazza San Marco, representing master craftspeople. The showroom of **Zora da Venezia** (*Calle Larga 22 Marzo, San Marco, www.zorada venezia.com*) shows her creations in glass, including vases, glass flowers and picture frames.

Murano Glassworks
Chandeliers, all kinds of glasses, vases, jewellery, trinkets: from the most old-fashioned pieces to cutting-edge design, from the worst to the best, the cheap and cheerful to the exorbitant, the choice is vast in the many shops of the **Fondamenta Vetrai** and **Fondamenta Manin**, not to mention the factory shops.
If you seek authentic Murano glass made only here, the following produce glass only in Murano (they do not add imports to their line or have their designs made

elsewhere): Anfora, DinoRosin Arte Studio, Effe, Formia, Galliano Ferro, Gino Cenedese, Linea Vetro, NasonMoretti, Nuova Biemmeci, S.a.l.i.r, and Seguso Viro. The **Glass Museum** (*see p92*) also has a small shop.

Venini – *Fond. Vetrai 50*. Objects by leading Italian designers such as **Ettore Sottsass**.

Berengo – *Fond. D. Manin 68A*. Glass sculptures by renowned artists.

Nason Moretti – *Fond. Manin 52*. Even without buying, a visit to one of the workshops (*fornaci*) that are open to the public means you can admire the skill of the craftsmen and watch the piece taking shape and acquiring its colours in the furnace-like atmosphere as the glassblower manipulates the heated glass using his tweezers.

Davide Penso (*Fondamenta Riva Longa 48*), an instructor at the glassmakers' school, uses *perle a lume* technique that makes for attractive jewellery.

Stationery

Fine paper and a handwritten letter becomes rarer by the day, but the recipient is ever more delighted. You might also select a finely bound journal to record your travel impressions and drawings. A number of shops sell beautifully embossed or marbelised paper. The famous Venetian marbled paper can be bought in many shops in the city, including **Alberto Valese's** (*3471 Santo Stefano, San Marco, www.albertovalese-ebru.com*), and in San Polo, **Paolo Pelosin** works in his cramped workroom at Il Pavone (*Campiello del Meoni, San Polo 178*). **Il Papiro** (*Calle del Piovan and Calle Della*

Bissa, San Marco) is a chain that has wrapping and writing paper, elegant glass pens, coloured inks and sealing wax. A graphomaniac will delight in the shops in Calle della Mandola, between Campo Manin and Campo Sant'Angelo, and Calle del Piovan, between Campo San Maurizio and Campo Santo Stefano. The **Legatoria Piazzesi** *(Campiello della Feltrina, between Santa Maria del Giglio and San Maurizio, www.legatoriapiazzesi.it)* stocks beautiful cards printed using old-fashioned Venetian methods. Traditional stationery can also be purchased at **Gianni Basso's** *(Calle del Fumo 5306, Cannaregio),* near the Fondamenta Nuove, near the *vaporetti.* The shop's friendly owner is able to produce a range of quality stationery, personal bookplates and business cards, embossed and printed using traditional methods.

Textiles

Known for its lovely velvets and brocades in fine silks, linen, and cotton, Venice is a treasure trove for a new wardrobe or for home design, including the accessories *(passamanerie)* like tassels and pom-poms. An accent pillow, drapes, or a Fortuny lamp might be just the finishing touch for a room.

Fashion

The Venetian love of fine textiles certainly extends to their own adornment – and Venetians are an elegant lot. Venice is a great city for a total makeover, for men or women, and from head to toe. Look for fine-quality leather, from purses to shoes and gloves.

Lace

The art of lacemaking is vanishing. Skilled artisans are few and modern times have brought reduced demand. Venice has a school established for those who wish to learn and carry on the lacemaking tradition. You can find lace for trim, in clothes, tablecloths, and other items.

Curtains, tablecloths and a variety of products made of lace can be found at **Capricci e Vanità** in Dorsoduro *(San Pantalon, north of Campo Santa Margherita).* Doilies, handkerchiefs, trim, camisoles and bedspreads: the choice is vast in **Burano** in the rows of shops along the Fondamenta S. Mauro and Via Baldassare Galuppi, best seen after you visit the museum, as quality and point of origin varies considerably. Especially look for the lacemakers without a storefront, who sell their wares directly from their homes. They will make themselves known to you and perhaps will be working on a piece.

Dolls and Puppets

Valued for their fine details and the use of beautiful textiles in their costumes, Venice still has a few skilled dollmakers around; some will make dolls using your photographs or drawings, or will perform expert surgery on broken dolls. Dolls and puppets come in all shapes and sizes at **Carta Alta** *(Campo San Barnaba, Dorsoduro, www.venicemaskshop.com)* and **Il Sogno Veneziano** *(Calle Longa, San Croce).*

MUST DO

Works of Art

Galleries in Venice represent emerging artists, as well as the famous, from offbeat to elegant. You'll find shops all around Venice, with the biggest concentration around San Marco, but also check around the Accademia and other museums.

An excellent selection of paintings and artwork, many not surprisingly on Venice itself, can be found at the colourful **Itaca Bottega Artistica**, *(Calle delle Bande 5267/A, Castello, www.itacavenezia.it)*, near Santa Maria Formosa.

Food and Wine

Venice offers a superb selection and array of food, from breakfast breads and pastries to meats and salami, cheeses, fish, chocolate, special lagoon vegetables and fruit, coffee and beautiful desserts. Local wines come from as close as Mazzorbo to other parts of the Veneto region or nearby Friuli Venezia-Giulia. Prosecco, Amarone, Tocai are to name just a few. A good sommelier or wine shop can give you plenty of suggestions.

Model Boats

The shop window of **Gilberto Penzo's** near I Frari *(Calle Seconda dei Saoneri 2681, San Polo, www. venetia.it/boats/penzo_eng.htm)* displays a fine collection of model boats, gondolas and *bricole* made from wood. The shop also sells model kits, construction plans, reliefs of historical constructions, rowlocks and nautical ex-votos.

Pasta

Pasta of all colours, shapes and sizes can be purchased at **Rizzo's** *(Calle dei Fabbri, www.rizzostore.com)*.

Confectionery

Volpe *(in the Ghetto, Cannaregio)* sells a selection of Jewish bread and pastries. Pasticceria **Toletta** *(on the street of the same name, Dorsoduro)* tempts browsers with pastries and candies.

Districts

Piazza San Marco

🕙 **A bit of advice** – There are numerous boutiques selling Murano glass under the arcades of the Procuratie. The lace shops are concentrated around Piazzetta dei Leoncini.

Libreria Aqua Alta B1 – *Campiello del Tintore (Calle Longa di S. Maria Formosa)– Castello 5176*. An unusual bookshop in a building overlooking a little garden and a canal. A real Ali Baba's cave for book lovers, where you will find titles in all genres and all languages. Also rents out a few B&B rooms.

For an upscale male makeover, head to **Ermenegildo Zegna** *(Bocca di Piazza San Marco 1242)*, where the suits are exquisite. Damasks, silks and velvet for drapes, pillows and bedcovers are at **Ca'Nova** *(San Marco 4601)*. Make way for cashmere at **Loro Piana** *(San Marco Ascensione 1301)* or at **Malo** *(San Marco 2359)*. Try **Jade Martine** *(San Marco 1645)* for beautiful Italian and French lingerie.

Dea Fashion *(Calle dei Fabbri 932)* sells gloves made in Naples. If you need to gild something, whether a frame or an ornament, take it to gilders **Gianni and Alberto Cavalier** *(Santo Stefano 2863/A)*, who will turn it to gold or accent it.

SHOPPING

117

Le5Venice Contemporary Art Gallery *(Campo Sa Fantin, San Marco 1895/6)* has a friendly, quirky atmosphere, and often has some wearable art. Lady Gaga isn't likely to make an appearance here, but if you need comfortable quality walking shoes, try **Calzature Bonato** *(Calle delle Bande)*.

Venetia Studium has several shops *(San Marco 2425, 723, 4753)* that sell Fortuny lamps, as well as velvet scarves and stoles.

Atelier Flavia *(Santa Marini)* sells historically accurate costumes for the serious buyer, by appointment only *(www.veniceatelier.com)*.

Rialto

Clothes

Buosi *(San Bortolomeo)* is a Venetian tradition that has kept men looking dapper since 1897; they make clothes to measure, have a quality selection of ready-to-wear and handsome neckties. **Vladis Shoes** *(San Polo 247/48)* sells stylish and quirky shoes, some made in Venice, also at another shop *(Cannaregio 2340)*.

Food shopping

Markets – **Fruit and vegetables**: Campo S. Giacomo and along the Grand Canal; **fish**: La Pescheria; **meat**: Campo delle Beccarie. Markets are held every morning, up to around 1pm, and may also be open in the afternoon. Aside from their colourful atmosphere, the markets are great for those renting apartments who want to stock up on fresh produce.

Casa del Parmigiano B1– *Campo Cesare Battisti (next to Campo della Pescaria)* – *S. Polo 214*. As well as parmesan in all its forms, you will find all kinds of Italian cheeses in this gourmet food shop, from *pecorino toscano* to *gorgonzola*. Other treats on offer include San Daniele ham, balsamic vinegar, olive oil and artisanal pasta. In short, a food lover's paradise. You will also find a number of shops to whet your appetite along the **Ruga Vecchia San Giovanni**.

Traditions

Legatoria Polliero A2 – *Campo S. Polo*. A genuine workshop where you can have your favourite books bound in marbled Venetian paper or simply buy new blank books for your travel diaries.

Vivaldi Store B2 – *Campo S.Bartolomio*. As its name suggests, this record shop is devoted to Venetian music and musicians. With themed records (lute, *clavicimbalo*, "duels" (organ duets), sonatas and madrigals), and recordings of works by local composers (including the "Red Priest", of course), you will find the whole catalogue of the local label Nalesso Records here.

Masks – Along the very busy route leading from the Rialto market to the station (Ferrovia), you will find numerous mask shops and workshops.

La Fenice

Fashion

Salvatore Ferragamo, **Gucci**, **Bulgari**, **Versace**, **Prada**… The biggest names in Italian fashion are to be found on Calle Larga 22 Marzo and the Salizada San Moisè.

Borsalino C1 – *Calle del Lovo (Campo S. Salvador), S. Marco 4822*. Legendary hats.

Giuliana Longo C1 – *Calle del Lovo, S. Marco 4813*. A family business since 1901, this tiny hat shop has lovely variety, from wool felt or velvet with feathers, to the famous hand-made Montecristi panama hats, or a reasonably priced doge's hat for Carnival.

JB C1 – *Calle del Lovo, S. Marco 4821*. Gloves in all colours, with or without stitching, but always in leather.

Bookshops

Mondadori C1 – *Salizada S. Moisè, S. Marco 1345*. Wide choice of books about Venice.

Traditions

Il Papiro B1 – *Calle del Piovan (between S. Maurizio and S. Stefano), S. Marco 2764*. Marbled paper and writing accessories, a chain throughout Italy and beyond. Il Papiro in Calle della Bissa and Calle delle Bande.

La Ricerca B1 – *Ponte delle Ostreghe, S. Marco 2431*. One of Venice's famous stationery shops, selling items covered in marbled paper and beautiful letter-writing papers.

Il Prato B1 – *Calle delle Ostreghe (Campo S. Maria del Giglio), S. Marco 2456/9*. Leather goods (valet trays, wallets) and designer glassware offering a bit of a change from the Murano tradition.

Zora de Venezia B1 – *Calle Larga 22 Marzo (in a courtyard shaded by fig trees, at the end of a little street), S. Marco 2407*. Quality glassware and imaginative jewellery.

Santa Maria Novella A1 – *Salizada S. Samuele - S. Marco 3149 - www.smnovella.com*. This Florentine "dispensary of pharmaceutical perfumes" dates to 1612. After-shave creams and lotions, perfumes and eaux de toilette, all made to traditional recipes.

Mario Bevilacqua B1 – *Campo S. Maria del Giglio - S. Marco 2520*. Textiles and decorative trimmings, tie-backs, embroidery and velvet in the great tradition of Venetian fabrics, as you would expect from a business that has existed since 1700. Some items still woven on period looms. They even have some vintage Fortuny textiles here. Of his two Venice shops (another is in Castello), this is the most atmospheric.

Art galleries

Numerous galleries have opened up around Campo S. Maurizio and Campo S. Stefano, as well as in the little streets around S. Samuele and Palazzo Grassi.

La Salute

Museum Shop A1 – *Fond. Venièr dei Leoni*. The Guggenheim Collection shop: art books, reproductions, etc.

Claudia Canestrelli A1 – *Campiello Barbaro, Dorsoduro 364A*. More of a cabinet of curiosities than an antiques shop, where you will find high-quality objects such as prints, jewellery, trinkets, little votive offerings and much more.

Saverio Pastor A1 – *Fond. Soranzo or Fornace, Dorsoduro 341, www.forcole.com*. This authentic craftsman's workshop overlooks a *rio* just by the Peggy Guggenheim collection, in a charming, peaceful spot. Here, you will discover all the secrets of the *fórcola*, the unique angular rowlock in walnut wood that gives a gondola its manoeuvrability.

Santi Giovanni e Paolo

Librairie française BC3 – *Barbaria da Tole, opposite the Ospedaletto church, Castello 6358*. From Hugo Pratt to Philippe Sollers, and Jean d'Ormesson to Donna Leone, this is the place to go to find everything written about Venice in French (or translated into French).

Ca d'Oro

Bookshop at Ca' d'Oro B3 – *On the 1st floor of the gallery (access via the loggia).* As well as a large selection of books on Venice, you will also find "zoom art" magnifying lenses here, which are very useful for making out the details of the paintings in some of the churches.

Cannaregio and the Ghetto

👁 **A bit of advice** – Fruit and vegetable sellers set up their stalls morning and evening in the **Rio Terrà San Leonardo** and the *campo* of the same name. When Bill Clinton was elected US president, he was wearing a **Pierangelo Masciadri** tie *(Campo Bandiera e Moro)*, who also likes to work mythological figures into ties. **TSL** *(Cannaregio 1318)* sells lovely pillows and textiles, plus a few shawls and scarves. Buy a bag of coffee (beans or ground) from **Torrefazione Marchi** *(Cannaregio 1337)*, perhaps, then Venice's best coffee; their speciality, il Caffè della Sposa, is prepared daily from eight beans, each toasted separately, then blended (they advise to consume within 3 months or they will replace if you don't drink it by then!). **Pasticceria Dal Mas Cioccolateria** *(Lista di Spagna 149 150/A)* has excellent pastries and chocolates.

San Polo and Santa Croce

Marbled paper

Legatoria Polliero B2 – *Campo dei Frari (at the corner of Calle Passion), S. Polo 2995.* A bookbinder's workshop where you will find notebooks of various sizes covered with marbled paper.

Masks

🎭 **Tragicomica** B3 – *Calle del Traghetto Vecchio (between the campo and the S. Tomà vaporetto stop), S.Polo 2874 (also Calle dei Nomboli C2, S. Polo 2800). www. tragicomica.it.* Manufacture, sale and hire of masks and costumes.

Other traditions

Bottega Orafa B1 – *Calle del Tintor (near the Ponte del Megio), S. Croce 1839. www.orafaabc.com*. Rings, pendants, pens, sugar bowls: all the objects here are made of metal alloys using the formulas and technique of "mokume gane", the results of which are incorrectly termed "Damascus steel".
Fanny *(Calle dei Saoneri, Campo San Polo 2723)* sells saucy Neapolitan leather gloves with button accents (another shop is at Cannaregio 1647).
Il Mercante di Sabia B2 – *Calle dei Saoneri, S. Polo 2724.* Jewellery and pendants, metal objects, designer cups: a change from the usual Venetian gifts.
Gilberto Penzo B2 – *Calle 2a dei Saoneri, S. Polo 2681.* Models of gondolas, *vaporetti*, fishing boats, *fòrcole*, nautical literature. A must for all fans of boats and ships.

Sant'Elena and San Pietro

Marco Polo fine fabrics B2 – *Via Garibaldi, Castello 1696. www. marcopolotessuti.com.* Showroom.

SPAS

Given its reputation for sensuality and luxury, the relative scarcity of spas may come as a surprise to the Venice visitor. However, a good spa requires space, and in Venetian palaces, space is precious. Spas in Venice, therefore, are a relatively new phenomenon.

Venetian spas?

The closest spas are in luxury hotels on the Giudecca Canal, although a Lido hotel (*see below*) managed to fit a Thai spa into its Art Nouveau space. Spas are and will remain a rarity in Venice. On the other hand, the words "gym" or "fitness centre" might make a Venetian shudder, with all the stairs, bridges and rowing opportunities that Venice provides. Some hotels reserve spa services exclusively for hotel guests, while others accept those from outside.

One word of advice: in Italy, unless you are speaking to someone who is fluent in English, the request for a "spa" may produce quizzical looks. "S.p.A." or "SpA" is a common Italian acronym for Società per Azioni, which refers to a joint stock or limited liability company (of which there are many thousands). More widely understood are *bagni termale* for thermal baths, or *centro benessere* for a wellness centre.

Giudecca
Palladio Spa

The **Bauer Palladio Hotel** (*see pp108, 119, 139*) claims that no other Venice city hotel has a spa on this scale. Set over two floors, eight rooms are dedicated to a special treatment each, including facials, Vitalis Bath (with Dead Sea minerals and muds) and sauna. The lounge area has three windows overlooking St Mark's Square. Open March–Nov.

 Hilton Molino Stucky

See p81. The unique feature here is the rooftop swimming pool. The wellness centre has a sauna, Turkish bath, hydro massage and a lounge to relax in, but with a time limit of two hours. Massages and beauty treatments are offered here or in guest rooms. Fitness centre.

Casanova Spa

Hotel Cipriani's spa (*see p81*) is named after Casanova who reputedly had trysts in what are now the hotel's gardens. There is a treatment cabin for massages for couples, bath with essential oils and flower petals, and pedicures. The fitness centre has a gym, steam bath, sauna and hair salon.

Lido
Lanna Gaia Wellness Center

The 1905 Lido hotel spa, **Grande Albergo Ausonia & Hungaria** *(Gran Viale S.M. Elisabetta, 28; 041 242 0060; www.hungaria.it)* offers northern Thai treatments, plus a Finnish sauna, steambath, aromatic steambath, Kneipp hydrotherapy, Jacuzzi, and lounge to relax in.

Thermal Baths

If you seek full spa treatments with thermal waters, just hop on the train toward Padova, where the towns of **Abano**, **Battaglia**, **Galzignano**, **Montegrotto** and **Teolo** offer treatments. The water source is in Monti Lessini in the foothills of the Alps.

CAFÉS

Sometimes the best travel memories are of sitting in a café – grand or simple, historic or modern, with a view or at an intimate corner – just watching the world go by. Visiting Venice involves a lot of walking "su e zo per i ponti" (up and down the bridges). An atmospheric café makes the perfect place to rest and to relish Venetian life.

Piazza San Marco

The Piazza San Marco is famous for its *gran caffès* and almost equally infamous for the prices they charge. Just bear in mind that when you pull up a chair in one of these establishments, you are not *just* buying a drink or a meal; rather you are taking up an exalted position in what Napoleon (supposedly) once called Europe's finest drawing room, where you are welcome to linger.

There are several cafés around San Marco but two are world-famous: the **Caffè Florian** *(www.caffeflorian.com)* and the **Grancaffè Quadri** *(www.quadrivenice)*. Opened in 1720, Caffè Florian is not only Venice's most venerable café but also the oldest in the country. Florian makes its own *gelato* and pastries, a better bet here than a full meal, although the delicate salmon sandwiches do nicely with some bubbly.

The Quadri, in its present incarnation, opened in 1830, though a coffee shop once traded on the same site – perhaps the first in Venice – which they claim dates to 1683. It's worth noting that from 2011 a new chef was in charge of the Ristorante Quadri upstairs, which means gourmets can enjoy a full meal. If you really want to push the boat out, take a seat outside either of these aristocratic *grand dames* (not forgetting to have a good look inside at some time during your visit, to admire their magnificent interiors),

Grancaffè Quadri

©Grancaffè Quadri

MUST DO

and enjoy the music of a live orchestra. Dancing in the piazza is encouraged, and many would argue it is the best way to get your money's worth.

Café Toto – Less elegant than the previous two; don't dine here, but they do make very good cappuccino and espresso. Their brew comes from a local *torrefazione* (coffee roaster), called Girani.

Just a few bridges north of San Marco, **Le Bistrot de Venise** makes a nice, quiet stop. The café near the stained-glass window and bar is more informal than its restaurant, and with a well-selected, extensive selection of wines by the glass.

Andrea Zanin Pasticceria – *San Marco 4589*. For pastries to go, the window display says it all, and it's good stuff.

Pizzeria Sansovino Forno – *San Marco 2628*. Andrea Soldà shows Venetians know how to make pizza, here as a quick stand-up snack of quality pizza by the slice.

Venchi Il cioccolato – *Calle dei Fabri San Marco 989*. For quality chocolates from Piemonte since 1878, the new twist added in 2011 is their excellent *gelateria*, with the superb *fondente* (bittersweet) or the *gianduia* made with hazelnuts from Piemonte. Venchi has other flavours, too, but it should be no surprise that chocolate is best!

Grand Canal

Sipping a coffee on the terrace of the **Monaco Hotel and Grand Canal** (*see p110*) opposite La Salute is a wonderfully relaxing experience. The same goes for the **museum café** (*see opposite and p53*) on the roof of the Peggy Guggenheim Collection.

Rialto

Café dell'Arte A1 – **Ca' Pesaro, Fond. Pesaro, S. Croce 2076**. At the end of the palazzo's *portego*, the museum café offers a terrace with views of the Grand Canal… which unfortunately disappear as soon as you sit down! Light meals available.

La Fenice

Le Café B1 – *Campo S. Stefano/ Calle dello Spezièr, S. Marco 2797*. On the street side is a good bakery selling cakes and biscuits, whilst on the *campo* side a large café with top-notch service makes breakfast on the square all the more enjoyable.

Accademia

Gelateria Nico B1 – *Zattere ai Gesuati, Dorsoduro 923*. Inside, this *gelateria* has the look of a rough-and-tumble bar, but outside tables face the Giudecca Canal, with the spectacle of passing boats and ships. Open 24 hours.

La Piscina B1– *Zattere ai Gesuati Dorsoduro 782*. With a spectacular terrace view of boats and ships from outside tables, this café succeeds in pleasing a diverse crowd, from their excellent, traditional home-made *gelato*, to salads or full meals for vegetarians as well as meat or fish lovers.

La Salute

Museum Café A1 – *In the Peggy Guggenheim gallery*. Access via the sculpture garden of the Peggy Guggenheim Collection. Relax on the terrace with art lovers, contemplate Guggenheim's colourful life, and plan your own famous collection.

CAFÉS

Santi Giovanni e Paolo

Rosa Salva B3 – *Campo SS. Giovanni e Paolo (at the end of Calle Bressana), Castello 6779*. Although the Rosa Salva name has only been over the door since 1995, this bar-*pasticceria-gelateria* dates to predecessor Angelo Ferluoch's day in 1922, and before that a cake shop in 1751. On the square facing the majestic church and the statue of the Condottiere Colleoni, enjoy fruit-based aperitifs, speciality cakes or fruit and chocolate yoghurts, as well as their hand-made ice cream, including their speciality based on cocoa.

Algiubagiò B1-2 – *Fond. Nuove, Cannaregio 5039. 041 523 60 84. www.algiubagio.net*. Whilst waiting for the *vaporetto* for the islands, why not take a break and enjoy a home-made ice cream? For those with a bigger appetite, they run the adjoining restaurant. This classy place has a nice terrace with views of the lagoon, and you can also enjoy tasty *panini* and *tramezzini* at the bar.

Italo Didovich B3 – *Campo di S. Marina, Castello 5509 (access from Campo dei Miracoli – take the little Calle Castetti then turn right)*. Discover true happiness when you taste Didovich's delicious *semifreddi*.

Ca' d'Oro

😊 **A bit of advice** – There are various little cafés where you can take a break on the *fondamente*.

Boscolo A3 – *Calle del Pistor, Cannaregio 1818*. Those with a sweet tooth will want to stop off at this enticing *pasticceria* offering delights such as *tartufini*, *pignolate* (pine nut tarts), *torta di ricotta*, *torrone morbido* (or *veneziano*: with chocolate and almonds)

and *focaccine veneziane* (figs, almonds and candied fruits), not to mention the famous *tiramisù*.

Cannaregio and the Ghetto

Azienda Agricola C2 – *Rio Terrà Farsetti, Cannaregio 1847A*. If there's one wine bar in Venice where you won't meet any tourists, then this is probably it!

Al Timon – *Fondamenta dei Ormesini*. Near the Ghetto, this tiny casual place has a handful of outdoor tables on a narrow canal, with good wines by the glass scribbled on the blackboard and a few hot dishes of the day.

Dolci Ebraici B2 – *Calle del Ghetto Vecchio, Cannaregio 1143. Unleavened bread, orecchiette di Amman*, almond pastries and all sorts of sweet treats flavoured with honey can be found in these two little kosher bakeries tucked away in the heart of the Ghetto.

Enoteca Do Colonne C2 – *Rio Terrà de Cristo, Cannaregio 1814C*. An appealing wine bar (also serving *crostini*), strategically located on the way to the San Marcuola *vaporetto*, away from the bustle of Rio Terrà San Leonardo.

I Frari and San Rocco

Al Prosecco B1 – *Campo S. Giacomo dall'Orio, S. Croce 1503*. An *enoteca* with a city-wide reputation and tables on a peaceful *campo*. Naturally, the famous sparkling wine made in the Veneto takes pride of place, but you can pair it with a selection of cured meats or a few *crostini*.

Ai Nomboli B2–C2 – *Rio Terà dei Nomboli, near Casa Goldoni, S. Polo 2717. 041 523 0995*. A bar with an amazing range of delicious *tramezzini* to take away or eat in, perhaps on the little terrace facing the street, if you're lucky enough to find a space!

Pasticceria Rio Marin B2 – *Fta del Rio Marin, S. Croce 784.* With its magnificent *tiramisù*, house specialities with strawberries and other red berries, chocolate *crostate* and more, the window of this cake shop is a magnet for food lovers. Even better, once you've chosen, you can eat in comfort at the tables, either inside or outside alongside the *rio*.

Pasticceria Dal Mas Cioccolateria – *Lista di Spagna 149 150/A.* Excellent pastries, like almond *kranz*, and fine chocolate make this stand-up affair worth a visit.

Camillo Marchi's Caffè Costarica/ Torrefazione Marchi – *Cannaregio 1337.* This stand-up coffee bar merits a visit for the superb quality of coffee. Their house blend has eight varieties of beans, each roasted separately. Also other beans to sample. Sip a coffee or buy some bags to give as gifts or souvenirs (and if you don't use your beans, ground or whole, after three months they will replace them).

Cioccolateria Vizio Virtù B3 – *Calle del Campaniel or Givran or Grimani (just by Campo S. Tomà), S.Polo 2898A. www.viziovirtu.com.* A chocolate specialist: truffles (*tartufi*), chocolate with dates, passion fruit, figs, macaroons… a must for any chocaholic!

Gelateria Alaska B1 – *Calle Larga dei Bari, S. Croce 1159.* For those with a taste for ice cream and adventure: choices range from green melon to carrot or fennel. But this *gelateria* captures flavours of all kinds, including its traditional *gelati*.

I Carmini

Bar Ai Artisti C1 – *Campo S. Barnabà/Calle del Traghetto, Dorsoduro 2771.* This little bar sets out its tables on the *campo* facing the church, making it the ideal place for people-watching with a coffee or a *sprítz*.

Caffè Margaret Duchamp B1 – *Campo S. Margherita, Dorsoduro 3019.* One of several large cafés on this *campo*. Design-led décor and a terrace on the square.

Il Lido

Villa Laguna – *Via S. Gallo 6.* The hotel boasts a pleasant garden and sublime views of the lagoon, Venice and S. Giorgio Maggiore. Refreshments, hot drinks or aperitifs are available depending on your mood and the time of the day, and can be supplemented by light meals (snacks and salads).

Burano

Pasticceria Constantini – *San Martino Sinistro, Burano 282.*
Pasticceria Carmelina Palmisano – *Via Baldassare Galuppi 355.* These two bakeries feature local specialities, *bussolai buranelli*: sweet biscuits that come in various shapes (rings and S-shapes being the most common).

Mazzorbo

Antica Trattoria alla Maddalena – *Mazzorbo 7/B.* This trattoria also doubles as island bar for the locals and the outside tables are open for breaks in between meal hours.

Murano

Bar Gelateria al Ponte – *Riva Longa 1/c.* Once the tourists drift away, locals exchange news at the tables set along the quiet canal.

CAFÉS

RESTAURANTS

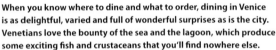

When you know where to dine and what to order, dining in Venice is as delightful, varied and full of wonderful surprises as is the city. Venetians love the bounty of the sea and the lagoon, which produce some exciting fish and crustaceans that you'll find nowhere else.

Luxury	<60€	*Moderate*	20€–40€
Expensive	40€–60€	*Inexpensive*	>20€

Dining Options

A **bàcaro** *(pl.bàcari)* or **osterìa** *(pl. osterie)* is a very simple type of establishment that serves wine and a simple food menu. A *cichetteria* serves *cichèti* and wine, sometimes a few rice or pasta dishes. An **enoteca's** *(pl. enotèche)* purpose is to sell wine, but because generally Italians do not drink wine unless they also eat something, you can count on at least some snacks, simple platters, or a hot dish to accompany the wines.

A **pizzeria** (and sometimes *forno*) is an establishment with a pizza oven (look for woodburning), and some specialise only in pizzas. The distinction among various terms for establishments is blurring in Italy. Traditionally a **locanda** is an "inn" or a "guesthouse", and may have a few rooms; a **trattorìa** meant modest but plentiful food, but now may be very upscale; or a **taverna** had dining, and finally, a **ristorante** was a bit more formal. Now it's best to consult the menu.

Our Selection

We are keen to include all areas of Venice, so that you can combine exploration of the city with gastronomic discoveries. This is why we have included some bars, *enoteche* and *bàcari* in the restaurant section if they have a place where you can sit down and order some cooked food.

Our prices reflect the cost of a two-course meal with a carafe of wine.

Business Hours

Most restaurants keep fairly restricted hours and are earlier than in Rome and the South: lunch *(pranzo)* is eaten between midday and 2pm, and dinner *(cena)* from 7.30–8pm onwards. A few places in tourist areas either offer continuous service or some options in between.

When hunger strikes outside of traditional mealtimes, *bàcari* typically have been a resource, often open all day, but may close quite early (around 9pm).

Sit-down Meals...

Some places advertise tourist menus at bargain prices, sometimes quite aggressively. Check exactly what is included in the price before you sit down, and do not expect too much in the way of originality or quality. It would be a shame to look no further, because Venetian cuisine offers a wealth of flavours. You can eat very well in Venice without making a huge hole in your budget. Some down-to-earth restaurants frequented by working people and students offer dishes that are traditionally as tasty as the portions are large. Some high-end restaurants offer a reduced menu or tasting menus at lunchtime at reasonable prices.

👉 **A bit of advice** – Prices for fish are sometimes given per 100g *(etto)*. An extra amount for bread and the cover charge *(pane e coperto)* is usually added to your bill, and service is not always included.

…or Light Bites

At the bar

Standing at the bar of one of the city's *bàcari*, you can eat *cichèti* or *crostini* – little snacks like Spanish tapas. This Venetian tradition is ideal for a quick bite at lunchtime and even more so at aperitif time. Every evening, young people meet up to enjoy the ritual of a *giro di òmbra* (wine bar crawl): *òmbra* is dialect for a very inexpensive glass of wine served at the bar to wash down your *cichèti*.

Take away

Panini and **tramezzini** are takes on the sandwich and do a good job of banishing the midday hunger pangs. Italian creativity can be seen in fillings such as *prosciutto crudo* with artichoke hearts, mortadella, anchovies and cheeses. Also, don't forget that a **pizza al taglio** (pizza slice) makes an excellent snack.

👉 **A bit of advice** – You usually go first to the cash desk to pay for what you want to eat or drink. (Some items like *pizza al taglio* or cured meats or cheeses must first be weighed.) You can then go to the counter to collect your purchase in exchange for the receipt.

Food and Wine

Venice has traded with the world since the dawn of time; throughout its history the city has therefore been cosmopolitan in every sense of the word. A thousand different ethnic types have crowded the streets and squares just as they have populated the pictures of Titian and Veronese. They have added colour to the Venetian scene, idiom and dialect to the vernacular language and, above all, exotic spice to the indigenous cultural and culinary traditions. The perfumes and fragrances exchanged in Venice have been blended and refined through time with more homespun scents and flavours. The multitude of foreign merchants (except for Chinese who increasingly are occupying more shops and restaurants) has been replaced with crowds of tourists, and so the alchemy continues.

Social history has also played its part: both aristocratic refinement and solid peasant cooking have left their mark. Tourism has nurtured a demand for restaurants that alternate between luxurious and anonymous "tourist" fare, but the age-old rhythm of the city and the convivial habits of its citizens still survive and flourish: **un ombra di vin** (literally, a wine taken in the shade) accompanied by a **cichetto** (a tasty morsel) or three, consumed in a **bacaro**, is one of life's small daily luxuries for the locals.

Cichèti (the plural of *cichetto*) comprise all kinds of foods from sliced fried vegetables to delicious garlic meatballs *(polpette)*, squid, salt-cod and prawns to mini pizzas and bruschettas.

When ordering "*un ombra*", that will bring forth a glass of the house white. If you want red, request a *rosso*.

Seafood

Venetians are especially proud of their seafood. A traditional plate of *antipasto* offers a chance to relish a wonderful selection. Local shellfish include **caparòssoli** (*vongole verace*/clams), **i caparossoli in cassopipa** (clams sautéed in white wine), long razor clams (*razzoi*), **peòci** (*cozze*/mussels), *lumache di mare* (sea snails), **canòce** (*cannocchia*, delicious odd-looking whitish grey Adriatic spiny sea mantis), *cape sante* (scallops), **moéche** (softshell small green lagoon crabs, exquisite fried and eaten whole), as well as **granseole** (spider crab). *Seppie al nero*, cuttlefish in its own ink, is a rich-tasting dish served with pasta, rice, or spongy yellow polenta which gradually becomes black as it absorbs the ink! The fish come in many varieties, too. Fish from the Adriatic is often served raw, fried or grilled. In spring, it is accompanied by **castraùre** (young artichokes sliced and served raw), a delicious purple artichoke from Sant'Erasmo and other lagoon islands. Eel (*anguilla*, or **bisàto** in dialect), less frequently on menus, is served either broiled or poached. Crudo, raw fish, is popular. For fried fish, don't miss the *fritolin* (fish fryer), who serves them wrapped in a paper cone to absorb the oil. As a *primo* or starter, **bigoi in salsa** (thick, coarse spaghetti served with lightly fried onions and anchovies) is one of the most popular first courses (after which you may be too full to eat any more!). In Northern Italy rice is more popular than pasta so you can expect to see many types of risotto on the menu, plus polenta made from cornmeal. These are made with meat and/or fresh vegetables (**primavera**), grown locally in market gardens, or with fish, or **'in tecia'** – with cuttlefish. Vinegar was traditionally used for pickling and preparing fish or seafood for long sea voyages, a tradition that remains: prepared with onions, **in saòr**, this delicious sweet-and-sour dish is most commonly made with **sarde** (*sardine*) or shrimp. Another truly typical dish is **bacalà mantecato**, salt-cod laboriously beaten with milk to a smooth cream, and served with polenta. It is often served as a *cichetto*, on bread or perhaps a cracker.

Meat dishes

One of the most traditional *secondi* or main courses is **figà àea venessiana** (*fegato alla veneziana*/calf's liver and onions often finished with a splash of white wine), a combination created in Venice but now popular everywhere. The defining factor for Venetians, however, is how gently and slowly the onion is cooked. Another Venetian invention, **carpaccio**, very thinly sliced raw beef, is served cold with mayonnaise, mustard sauce, or drizzled with olive oil. It is credited as an invention of Harry's Bar in Venice, where in 1950 the countess Amalia Nani Mocenigo requested raw meat to improve her health. It was named *carpaccio* by Giuseppe Cipriani, the bar's owner at the time, because the colours reminded him of those of the great Venetian painter.

A favourite way of preparing veal in summer is **vitello tonnato** – veal in a tuna sauce, a surf-and-turf concoction that is always served cold.

In autumn and winter, don't miss *selvaggina*, many varieties of water fowl, including *anatra* (duck), perhaps stuffed or in *saòr*.

Soups

Economical and flavoursome country cooking includes **panàda veneziana**, a wholesome soup made with bread, garlic, oil, bay leaf and Parmesan cheese, or **pastissàda**, a concoction of green vegetables, cheese, sausage, pasta or polenta bound together traditionally to use up leftovers. These are more likely to show up in someone's home than on a restaurant menu.

Zuppa di Pesce is a wholesome and hearty soup of fish.

Pasta e fasioi is a delicious thick northern Italian pasta and white bean soup. *Risi e bisi* is rice and peas with a bit of wild fennel, pancetta and parsley, a traditional San Marco feast-day dish. *Radicchio*, especially that from Treviso, has been popular since the 15C. In autumn *zucca* (pumpkin) is popular with rice, roasted, or boiled. Venetians also prepare potatoes in a variety of ways.

Dolci

For dessert, try the famous **tiramisu**, another Venetian invention combining chocolate, coffee, cream, mascarpone cheese and sometimes a twist on tradition with brandy or other liqueur. **Pannacotta,** literally cooked cream, is a delicious dessert with a texture very similar to crème caramel, usually served with wild berries, or perhaps a caramel or chocolate sauce. Don't overlook *gelato*, although it's increasingly difficult to find good artisanal *gelato* made with fresh,

first-rate ingredients. Another very Venetian custom is to serve **baìcoli** biscuits which should be dunked in drinking chocolate or a *passito* dessert wine; other kinds of biscuits and sweets are **bussolài**, moulded into ring or "S" shapes, called *essi buranèi*. The **Veneziana**, a kind of brioche generally served for breakfast, may be covered with a custard or chopped almonds and sugar. For Carnival there are typical Shrove Tuesday fried pancakes, **frìtole**, made from a dough flavoured with raisins and pine nuts. **Pìnsa**, a biscuit flavoured with fennel seeds, raisins, dried figs and candied peel, is a speciality baked at Christmas or Epiphany.

Coffee, whether it's to start a day, to recharge, or relax after dinner, is excellent in Venice, which has some of its own artisanal brands right in the city. Venice claims it was the first in Italy to roast coffee and to open coffee bars. Perhaps best is Marchi in Cannaregio not far from the train station, but there are others: also very good is Girani, roasted in Santa Croce but served in exclusive cafés and restaurants around the city; India, roasted in Dorsoduro; and Doge which has transferred its facilities to Padova but can be sampled in the Musei Veneziani coffee bars.

Saluti!

The most common drink in Venice (and the Veneto), after *un ombra*, is a **spritz**, which is a white wine with a dash of bitters, garnished with lemon or orange peel, and soda water. If you order a spritz you should specify *com Campari* or (more normally) *com Aperol,* or with *Cynar. Reminder: As with other cities in Italy, when having a coffee*

or cocktails in bars, if you sit down usually the price is considerably higher than if you drink while standing. It's more worthwhile to sit when you know you can linger, than when you just want to grab something on the run and continue sightseeing. You can always enquire before ordering by specifying "al bar" or "a tavola".
Venice's most famous cocktail is the **Bellini**, one-quarter measure of fresh white peach juice to three of *Prosecco*, a dry Italian sparkling white wine; other variations include the **Rossini**, made with strawberry juice; the **Mimosa**, with orange juice; and the **Tintoretto** with pomegranate juice added. Ernest Hemingway was a frequent visitor to **Harry's Bar**, where he would order his own special cocktail, the **Montgomery**, named after the famous general. It was made with one measure of vermouth to 15 measures of gin and is served only by that particular establishment. Lighter and effervescent is a refreshing glass of **Prosecco**, the Veneto's very own sparkling wine made from Prosecco grapes; this 19C invention was an alternative to the more costly and lengthy method used in making Champagne.
Wine is a must with meals, and plenty of wines come from the Veneto and nearby regions. Mazzorbo now produces Dorona, a golden white wine. Friuli Venezia Giulia is often associated with whites like Picolit and even some Tocai, while the Veneto has Soave made from Garganega grapes, often blended with others. The Veneto has a good variety of reds and from the Valpolicella zone alone there are Amarone, Recioto, and Valpolicella, often

using the same varietals of grape, but with different methods that produce very different wines. Many other local reds and whites are made in the Veneto and Friuli, as well as local wines made from international varieties of grapes.

PIAZZA SAN MARCO

😀 **A bit of advice** – For other eating options in and around the square, see **Cafés** (*p122*) and the entries under **La Fenice** (*p133*) and Schiavoni and **Arsenale** (*p136*).

Moderate

All'Acciughetta B1 – *Campo SS. Filippo e Giacomo, Castello 4357. 041 522 4292.* The sidewalk tables of this trattoria are often packed with tourists, while the rustic dining room tends to be favoured by locals. Food quality has slipped in recent years, but their "pranzo dei operai", lunch specials for workers, are quite reasonable.
Alla Rivetta B1 – *Salizada S. Provolo, Between St Mark's Square and Campo S. Zaccaria, Castello 4625. 041 528 7302.* A wide choice of *cichèti* right by S. Zaccaria.
Enoteca Mascareta Lorenzon B1 – *Calle Longa di S. Maria Formosa, Castello 5183.* A wine bar serving up plates of *cichèti* (marinated fish, ham and cheese, platter of Italian cheeses) or hot dishes (allow €35 for a full meal) in an inviting atmosphere.
Al Mascaròn B1 – *Calle Lunga S.Maria Formosa, Castello 5225. 041 522 5995.* A renowned *osteria* serving authentic cuisine. Best to book ahead!

Expensive

Bistrot de Venise A1 – *Calle dei Fabbri, S. Marco 4685. 041 523 6651. www.bistrotdevenise.com.*

A chic bistro-style lounge with an elegant zinc bar, dining room, and sidewalk seating. Sergio's passion for Venetian culinary history has put a few historic dishes on the menu, such as *bisato de vale*, roast eel flavoured with oranges in wine, cinnamon and bay. Most of the menu explores traditional and contemporary cuisine. Some 500 wines are available here by the glass, more by the bottle.

Alle Testiere B1 – *Calle del Mondo Nuovo (between Salizada S. Lio and Campo S. Maria Formosa), Castello 5801. 041 522 7220. www.osteriaalletestiere.it. Closed Sun and Mon*. This little restaurant is renowned for its seafood and its bold flavour combinations: from John Dory with citrus fruit to *capesante* (scallops) with liqueur or *canestrelli* with lemon and mint. For less adventurous tastes, there is also a selection of grilled fish.

Luxury

Quadri A2 – *Piazza S. Marco 10 (upstairs). 041 522 2105. www.quadrivenice.com. Closed Mon (Nov–Jan)*. In the refined red-walled rooms overlooking St Mark's Square and bedecked with Murano glass chandeliers, this restaurant brought in a new chef in 2011, who emphasises new twists plus some traditional favourites.

Do Leoni B2 – *Riva degli Schiavoni, Castello 4171. www.londrapalace.com. 041 520 0533. Closed Jan*. The restaurant of the Hotel Londra Palace is another Venetian institution. Panoramic terrace in summer with unobstructed view of the lagoon. Booking essential.

Harry's Bar A2 – *p110* – Don't overlook Harry's bar for a meal. Prices are extravagant, but quality is high. Arrigo Cipriani personally inspects his own suppliers, going up to Norway to procure salmon and so on. The menu leans toward Venetian tradition. Sunday's *osso buco* makes good, hearty comfort food. Upstairs has a view of **St Mark's Basin**. Best to dress the part or you won't find a seat in these musical, magical chairs.

RIALTO
Grand Canal

🔎 **A bit of advice** – On either side of the canal, downstream from the Rialto, on the **Fondamenta del Vin** or the **Riva di Ferro**, there are numerous restaurants with terraces, more renowned for their views than for their cuisine.

Bàcari crawl
Around the edges of the market, you will find numerous little bars, some of which appear in our selection (Vini da Pinto, Bancogiro, All'Arco) as they are also restaurants. You can adopt the Venetian habit of sampling various *cichèti*, often delicious, accompanied by a glass of house wine in each place, gradually building up to a meal on the move.

Inexpensive
Left bank

Rosticceria Gislon B2 – *Calle della Bissa, S. Marco 5424*. Self-service style, but high quality, with a wonderful choice of Venetian dishes! You can eat at the bar, take a seat at one of the tables on the ground floor or sit down in more comfortable surroundings upstairs.

Al Rusteghi B2 – *Corte del Tintor (access from S. Bartolomeo via Calle de la Bissa and the sottoportego on the left), S. Marco 5513. 041 523 2205. Closed Sun.* You will find excellent panini here, or you could take a seat at one of the tables in the little courtyard and enjoy an *òmbra* with a salad.

Right bank

The Erberia is a particularly lively part of Venice both at lunchtimes and in the evenings. With its lively atmosphere, it's also the perfect place to enjoy an *òmbra* with some *cichèti*.

Al Mercà B1 – *Campo Bella Vienna (Erberia), S. Polo 213.* A place to make you feel like a real Venetian. Order a drink at the tiny bar facing onto the *campo*, choose from one of the many delicious *panini* and hang out with the locals taking a break before going back to the office. An enjoyable experience!

Pronto Pesce A1 – *Pescheria Rialto, S. Polo 319 (near Campo delle Beccarie). www.prontopesce.it. Closed Sun and Mon.* A little place with a nice menu of *cichèti*, or you could also try the delicious fish dishes. On Saturdays at 1pm, Venetians flock here for the *risotto di pesce*, with tourists hard on their heels!

All'Arco B1 – *Calle dell'Occhialer (a stone's throw from the Ruga S. Giovanni via the Sottoportego dei Do Mori), S. Polo 436. 041 520 5666. Closed Sun.* This tiny place is known for its *crostini*, has an excellent choice of wines and is always packed when the market is in full flow.

Cantina Do Mori B1– *S. Polo 429.* Authentic *bàcaro* dating from 1462 and serving up very good *cichèti*.

Antico Dolo B2– *Rugo Rialto. S.Polo 778. 041 522 6546. Closed Sun.* The little red-walled dining room of this *osteria* offers tripe, *crostini*, polenta and *bacalà mantecà* at mealtimes, along with a tasting menu. *Òmbre* and *cichèti* throughout the day.

Vini Da Pinto B1 – *Campo delle Becarie, S.Polo 367. 041 522 4599.* The time to come for a glass of white wine with a few *cichèti* is during your morning shopping trip. Otherwise, the place has succumbed to the lure of the tourist trade and the dishes served at the tables in the square are nothing special.

Bancogiro B2 – *Campo S. Giacomo, S. Polo 122-123. Closed Mon.* "Bank exchange" might seem a peculiar name for an *enoteca*! But centuries ago this *palazzo* was the site of one of Venice's first banks. Wine from the bar, plus the little dining room upstairs serves unpretentious but flavoursome food. Try the "pregnant" (stuffed) sardines!

Moderate
Left bank

Al Vagon B1 – *Sottoportego del Magazen (close to Campo SS.Apostoli), Cannaregio 5597. 041 523 7558. Closed Tue.* Honest Venetian food in a nicely turned-out dining room beside a canal, a little way from the crowds heading from the Rialto to the station, beneath a *sottoportego*.

Right bank

Al Nono Risorto A1 – *Sottoportego de la Siora Bettina (Campo S. Cassiano, beyond the rio of the same name), S. Croce 2338. 041 524 1169. Closed Wed.* A modest place, with a shaded terrace facing onto the *campo*. The pasta and pizza are popular with the locals.

Pane, Vino e San Daniele A1 – *Calle Boteri, S. Polo 1544. 380 410 8446 (mobile). Closed Mon.* Like its sister establishment on Campo de l'Anzolo San Rafaele *(see I Carmini)*, this place is devoted to the famous *prosciutto crudo* from Piemonte. An attractive, rustic dining room offers a choice of *cichèti* and dishes of the day on the chalk board.

Poste Vecie B1 – *Rio delle Beccarie/Pescheria Rialto, S. Polo 1608. 041 721 822. Closed Tue.* A little wooden bridge leads to this trattoria known as the "old post office", which it once was. It's also the city's oldest trattoria, dating back to the 16C. The fine old dining room spills over into the garden with its pergola when the weather is good. The house speciality is *seppie* with polenta.

Expensive
Left bank

Al Graspo de Ua B2 – *Calle dei Bombaseri (between Campo S.Bortolomio and the Grand Canal), S.Marco 5094A. 041 241 3326. Closed Mon.* This restaurant nestling in a particularly narrow street has regained its former glory, which is good news for food lovers. Comes recommended, so it would be wise to book ahead.

Fiaschetteria Toscana B1 – *Salizada S. Giovanni Grisostomo (at the corner of Calle del Scaleter), Cannaregio 5719. 041 528 5281. Closed Tue and Wed lunchtime.* One of Venice's fine restaurants: don't miss *moeche*, lagoon crabs, when they are in season. Fish roasted in a salt crust is a speciality, but is also served grilled and fried. In these elegant surroundings,

you can also choose from dishes like sea bass risotto with *Prosecco* or *carpaccio di cèrvo* (venison) with balsamic vinegar, or even a juicy Chianina steak. And why not start with a few oysters or a plate of *scampi* with lemongrass and honey? Sidewalk dining on the *campo* when the weather is good.

Right bank

Vecio Fritolin A1 – *Calle della Regina (behind Campo S. Cassiano), S. Croce 2262. 041 522 2881. www.veciofritolin.it. Closed Mon and Tue lunchtime.* A traditional little place with a big reputation offering dishes based on produce from the nearby markets (try the swordfish tartare with olives and lemon), as well as delicious pasta made by the owner.

Alla Madonna B2 – *Calle de la Madonna, S. Polo 594. 041 522 3824. Closed Wed.* Traditional cuisine and a bustling atmosphere in its several rooms.

Luxury
Near Campo S. Polo

Da Fiore A2 – *Calle del Scaleter (from Campo S. Polo via the Calle and Ponte Bernardo), S. Polo 2202. 041 721 308. www.dafiore.net. Closed Sun and Mon.* Always cited by other restaurateurs as a top place to dine, this is one of Venice's two Michelin-starred restaurants. In a narrow little street a stone's throw from S. Polo.

La Fenice
Inexpensive

Al Volto B1 – *Calle Cavalli, connecting Campiello de la Chiesa (S. Luca) to the Grand Canal, S. Marco 4081.* An *enoteca* set in a peaceful *calle* where you can take a seat and enjoy the *ombre* and *cichèti*.

Moderate

Al Bacareto A1 – *Calle delle Boteghe (facing Campo S. Stefano, S. Marco 3447. 041 528 9336. www.osteriaalbacareto.com (in Italian). Closed Sat evening and Sun.* A long-standing restaurant serving up Venetian specialities, from the excellent, widely renowned *sarde in saòr* to *fegato* and *baccalà mantecato*. Or you could simply enjoy some *cichèti* at the bar with a glass of house wine.

Ai Assassini B1 – *Rio Terrà degli Assassini. S. Marco 3695. 041 528 7986. www.osteriaaiassassini.it. Closed weekends.* In a little street leading to the Rio San Luca, this small restaurant occupies the ground floor of an attractive building adorned with pairs of windows and serves a daily special to its regulars.

Expensive

Antica Carbonera C1 – *Calle Bembo (1st on the left after the Teatro Goldoni), S. Marco 4648. 041 522 5479. www.antica carbonera.it.* In a dining room decorated with objects and furniture from the yacht that belonged to Archduke Rudolph (of Mayerling fame!), you can enjoy classic Venetian cuisine, with both seafood and meat specialities.

Acqua Pazza B1 – *Campo S. Angelo, S. Marco 3808-3810. 041 277 0688. www.venicemasaniello.com. Closed Mon.* This restaurant serves Neapolitan cuisine (essentially fish and shellfish) and boasts an additional attraction: its tables on the *campo*, with a view of the leaning bell tower of S. Stefano.

Ai Mercanti C1 – *Corte Coppo, Calle dei Fuseri, S. Marco 4346A. 041 523 8269. Closed Sun and Mon lunchtime.* A restaurant on a quiet little square close to the Scala del Bovolo offers a light lunch at a reasonable price. Evening tasting menus of Venetian cuisine, sometimes with a twist.

Luxury

Antico Martini B1 – *Calle delle Veste/Campo S. Fantin, S. Marco 1983. 041 522 4121. www.antico martini.com. Closed Tue and Fri lunchtime.* On the same square as La Fenice, you will find one of Venice's traditions, serving local and international cuisine, although the service could be a little better organised.

La Caravella B1 – *Calle Larga 22 Marzo, S. Marco 2397. 041 520 8901. www.restaurantlacaravella.com.* An elegant restaurant and a stalwart of Venetian fine dining: in the dining room or the inner courtyard you will enjoy carefully prepared food. Reasonably priced lunch menus.

Accademia

🙂 **A bit of advice** – On the **Zattere**, several restaurants set out their tables on decks over the canal facing the island of Giudecca. The best traditional cuisine is at La Piscina, while Lineadombra serves stylish modern cuisine, and all have superb views!

Inexpensive

Al Bottegon (Cantine del Vino gia Schiavi) B1 – *S. Trovaso (opposite the church), Dorsoduro 992.* This *bàcaro* (wine bar) offers a wide choice of traditional *cichèti*. An unmissable experience and an ideal place for a quick meal standing at the bar.

Moderate

Taverna San Trovaso B1 – *S. Trovaso, Dorsoduro 1016. 041 520 3703. www.tavernasantrovaso.it. Closed Mon*. This pleasant canal-side *taverna*, a stone's throw from the Accademia, offers a wide choice of traditional dishes, such as *sepia* in its own ink served with polenta. Very popular with Venetians.

Ristorante San Trovaso B1– *Calle Nani, on the corner of Rio Terrà Carità. 041 523 0835. Closed Tue*. This offshoot of the *taverna* of the same name is located close by in a former warehouse and a courtyard.

Antica Locanda Montin A1 – *Fondamenta Borgo, Dorsoduro 1147. 041 522 7151. www.locandamontin.com*. This traditional *trattoria* on a quiet canalside boasts a pleasant courtyard shaded by an arbour. It also has a few rooms available to rent.

Ai Quattro Feri A1 – *Calle Lunga S. Barnaba, Dorsoduro 2754. 041 520 6978. Closed Sun*. In a bright little dining room with rustic décor, you can enjoy a peaceful meal thanks to the calm, attentive service. The "slow food" menu changes daily, according to what can be found in the markets. They only serve fish dishes. You choose your *antipasti* at the bar, then move on to generous main courses.

Expensive

La Rivista B1 – *Rio Terrà Antonio Foscarini, Dorsoduro 979A. 041 240 1425. Closed Mon*. This restaurant attached to the Hotel Ca' Pisani owes its name to a canvas painted in 1925 by Fortunato Depero for the *Rivista Illustrata del Popolo d'Italia*. The short menu focuses on local produce, cooked in a fairly innovative style. Service is both polished and friendly. Good list of local wines.

La Salute

Expensive

Cantinone Storico A1 – *Fond. Bragadin, Dorsoduro 660. 041 523 9577. Closed Mon*. A little dining room and some tables along the Rio di San Vio in good weather provide the setting for this pleasant restaurant, very popular with English-speaking customers and renowned for its fish and shellfish.

Luxury

Ai Gondolieri A1 – *Fond. de l'Ospedaleto (opposite the Ponte del Fornage, across the canal from the Guggenheim Museum), Dorsoduro 366. 041 528 6396. www.aigondolieri.com. Closed Tue*. The owner Giovanni knows his wines. Meat specialities include the famous Venetian-style *fegato* (liver) served with polenta, the beef filet with Refosco wine gravy and potato timbale, and home-made desserts including sorbets. A magnet for tourists, but still serves good food.

Zattere

La Piscina, *Dorsoduro 782. 041 241 3889. www.lacalcina.com*. The wood terrace hangs right at the Zattere's edge, perfect for ship- and boat-watching. The ample menu selection offers fish, meat, and good vegetarian dishes, plus pasta, salads, and the Zattere's best *gelato*, handmade the traditional way.

Lineadombra B1 – *Zattere ai Saloni, just before the Dogana,*

Dorsoduro 19. 041 241 1881. www.ristorantelineadombra.com. Closed Tue. A restaurant serving refined cuisine, either on the deck in fine weather or in the minimalist dining room: mille-feuille of scampi in *saòr* with apples, sea bass fillet with vanilla potatoes, or grilled *capesante* with yoghurt and saffron, as well as marinated raw fish and home-made pasta. Good wine list and attentive service. Alessio is a knowledgeable, friendly sommelier, so don't hesitate to ask for suggestions.

Schiavoni and Arsenale
Inexpensive

Alle Alpi da Dante A2 – *Corte Nova, Castello 2877. 041 528 5163.* This *osteria* far from the tourist haunts at the end of a *sottoportego* may not be much to look at, but it is popular with the locals. Enjoy a glass of house wine with a few *crostini* and practise your *venexiàn* on the regulars.

Moderate

Ai Corazzieri B2 – *Salizada dei Pignatèr (between the Arsenal and S.Giovanni in Bràgora), Castello 3839. 041 528 9859. Closed Thu.* A modest place serving up fish specialities in a simple but convivial atmosphere, full of people enjoying themselves.

Carpaccio A3 – *Riva degli Schiavoni, Castello 4088–4089. 041 041 528 9615. www.ristorantecarpaccio. com.* A few outdoor tables are at the base of the busy footbridge, while the cosy room upstairs has a view of St Mark's Basin in this friendly restaurant. The seafood antipasto is delicious, where the selection may include *crudo* (raw) shrimp, tuna and *mazzancolle*, or

tiny cooked shrimp on polenta, steamed razor clams, fish in *saòr* and other delicacies from the sea and lagoon. In season, try lagoon scallops with *tagliolini* (pasta); for the main course, fish poached, roasted or fried is good. For dessert, the ricotta cheesecake is good, or a tart made with home-made jam.

Da Remigio A2 – *Salizada dei Greci, Castello 3416. 041 523 0089. Closed Mon evening and Tue.* In an enclave of timeless little streets, the white-jacketed waiters of this small place provide old-fashioned service. The cuisine showcases Venetian specialities: *pesce spada affumicato* (carpaccio of smoked swordfish), *spaghetti all'amatriciana* (tomato sauce with smoked ham), *fritelle* with *zabaglione*… Good value for money.

Osteria ae Spezie – *Castello 3478/80 Salizzada San Antonin, Castello 3479. 041 241 2196. Winter closed Tue–Wed.* This small, busy informal place has a variety of options, but best just to ask what's good that day. Grilled *cappe lunghe* (razor shellfish) are delicious; tagliolini with shrimp and porcini mushrooms is a tasty coupling of the sea and forest. If there's a wait, just ask them to make a Bellini and sip it on the sidewalk. Limited but good selection of wines.

Expensive

Al Covo B3 – *Campiello della Pescaria, to the right of the Riva degli Schiavoni, just before Ca' di Dio, Castello 3968. 041 522 3812. www.ristorantealcovo.com. Closed Wed and Thu.* A highly regarded restaurant, even though, from the outside, nothing appears to set it apart from the rest. A little terrace on the square and an attractive dining room with exposed beams. Three tasting menus and renowned desserts. **Corte Sconta** B2 – *Calle del Pestrin, Castello 3886. 041 522 7024. Closed Sun and Mon*. In a little street right by the entrance to the Arsenale is one of the city's best restaurants, with a particular reputation for its sometimes unusual *antipasti*. The little dining room leads to a pleasant courtyard, always packed. Enjoy specialities such as the home-made pasta and excellent fish, either grilled or in sauce, and Lucia's well-selected wines. Booking is essential.

Luxury

🚢 **MET** A3 – *Riva degli Schiavoni, Castello 4149. 041 524 0034. www.hotelmetropole.com. Closed Mon*. In this superb restaurant with innovative cuisine – and two Michelin stars – the atmosphere is tranquil and service attentive, as befits prestigious Hotel Metropole, facing St. Mark's Basin.

Santi Giovanni e Paolo
Moderate

Al Ponte B2 – *Calle Larga G. Gallina, Cannaregio 6378. 041 5286157.* You will find this *osteria* just at the end of the bridge on your way from SS. Giovanni e Paolo. Specialities include salt cod with courgette flowers *(baccalà e fiori di zucca fritti)* or with olives and peppers. The million-dollar question is how to bag a table without turning up at opening time. **Un Mondo DiVino** B2 – *Salizada S. Canciano, Cannaregio 5984A*. A wonderful *bàcaro* in a former beef butcher's premises, which proudly proclaims its previous incarnation. The place gets very busy, and

not only will you not be able to sit down, you also risk having to tuck into your *òmbra* and *cichèti* in the street, along with most of your fellow customers. This is a small price to pay for the delicious food, however, especially since the atmosphere is extremely convivial. **Osteria-Enoteca Giorgione** A2 – *Calle dei Proverbi, Cannaregio 4582A. 041 522 1725. Closed Mon*. In a little street close to the *campo*, you can make a light meal of a plate of Venetian *cichèti* or *scampi fritti* in this place frequented by local gondoliers. A more substantial menu is served in the evening. **La Perla** A2 – *Rio Terrà dei Franceschi, Cannaregio 4615. 041 528 5175. Closed Sun*. Pizza aficionados will find a very wide choice at this decent pizzeria, including some unusual options. **Bandierette** C3 – *Barbaria delle Tole, Castello 6671. 041 522 0619. Closed Mon evening and Tue*. Near the *campo* and the Ospedaletto church, this purveyor of wines and spirits has a pleasant dining room where you can enjoy dishes such as the excellent *capesante* (scallops), with the added bonus of service with a smile. **Da Alberto** B2 – *Calle Piovan (extension of Calle Larga Giacinto Gallina leading from Campo SS. Giovanni e Paolo to the Chiesa dei Miracoli), Castello 5401. 041 523 8153. Closed Sun*. A minuscule dining room where you'll be offered the dish of the day written up on the slate. Either book or be prepared to wait. **Da Alvise** B2 – *Fond. Nuove, Cannaregio 5045A. 041 520 4185. Closed Mon*. A pleasant restaurant opposite the lagoon, not far from the *vaporetto* stop. Fish specialities.

Expensive

Vecia Cavana A2 – *Rio Terrà dei SS. Apostoli, Cannaregio 4624. 041 528 7106. www.marsillifamiglia.it*. Away from the busy thoroughfares, this restaurant is worth the detour for its traditional yet inventive cuisine: dishes like smoked swordfish or tuna, octopus mosaic or succulent aubergine *tortino* are followed by grilled fish (swordfish, sole, sea bass) or the more traditional *seppie in nero* served with the lightest polenta.

Osteria Boccadoro B2 – *Campiello Widman (from Campo S. Maria Nova via the narrow Calle Widman), Cannaregio 5405A. 041 521 1021. Closed Mon*. This huge place with a terrace on a nice little square offers a delicious selection of shellfish.

Ca d'Oro
Inexpensive

Ai Promessi Sposi B3 – *Calle dell'Oca (between Campo de SS. Apostoli and the Strada Nuova), Cannaregio 4367. 041 241 2747. Cichèti* and local cuisine served either in the little courtyard or the dining room with walls covered in classic 7-inch singles.

Alla Vedova B3 – *Calle Pistor (following on from the landing stage for the Ca' d'Oro vaporetto, beyond the Strada Nuova), Cannaregio 3912. 041 528 5324. Closed Thu and Sun lunchtime*. Another *bàcaro* that often gets packed: booking advised.

Moderate

Al Marinèr A2 – *Fond. Ormesini (near the Ponte dell'Aseo), Cannaregio 2679. 041 720 036*. In this very simple locals' trattoria in a down-to-earth district offers dishes like shrimp brochettes or stuffed mussels.

Da Rioba B2 – *Fond. della Misericordia, Cannaregio 2553. 041 524 4379. www.darioba.com (in Italian). Closed Mon*. On one of Cannaregio's fantastic canalside walkways blessed with the midday sun, this *osteria* has a few tables beside the water and a convivial atmosphere in the dining room when it fills up with regulars. Classy cuisine based on fresh fish, with home-made desserts to complete the picture. Good Italian wine list. Booking advised in the evenings.

Expensive

Il Paradiso Perduto B2 – *Cannaregio, 2540 - Fond. della Misericordia. 041 720 581*. Very well known in Venice for its authentic local cuisine, as well as a favourite meeting place for jazz enthusiasts.

Vini da Gigio B3 – *Fond. S. Felice, Cannaregio 3628A. 041 528 5140. www.vinidagigio.com. Closed Mon–Tue*. A restaurant overlooking a nice *rio* and occupying several little rooms with beamed ceilings. The tasty shrimp and pumpkin risotto is good to start. Fish is served marinated, grilled or in sauce, and there are meat dishes on offer as well. Laura makes good desserts. The place is popular with tourists, but the food is still good and has a good wine list. Booking recommended.

Al Fontego dei Pescatori B3 – *Sottoportego dei Tagiapera or Calle Priuli, Cannaregio 3726. 041 520 0538. www.alfontego.com. Closed Mon*. Whether you arrive via the *sottoportego* on the Rio San Felice or through the garden by the street, you will not regret your choice. Run by a former fishmonger in the market in this former warehouse where jazz plays in the background. Loris knows where to find the best local fish and shellfish, and how to serve it.

Anice Stellato A2 – *Fond. della Sensa, Cannaregio 3272. 041 720 744. Closed Mon.* This little restaurant entices people from all over Venice into a district far from the main thoroughfares. Fish lovers are lured by the innovative cooking and the subtle use of sometimes unexpected spices like the Star Anise of its name. The restaurant stays open between mealtimes, offering a choice of *cichèti*.

Cannaregio and the Ghetto
Moderate

Alla Fontana B2 – *Fond. di Cannaregio 1102 (on the corner of Calle delle Chioverette). 041 715 077. Closed Tue.* This wine bar frequented by a very local crowd also operates a little restaurant serving tasty food. Tables on the canalside when weather is good.

Ai Canottièri A2 – *Fond. di S. Giobbe, Cannaregio 690. 041 717 999. Closed Sun evening and Mon.* A little café serving up daily specials to hordes of students from the nearby university.

Da A'Marisa A2 – *Fond. di S. Giobbe, Cannaregio 652. 041 720 211. Closed Mon evening and Tue evening*. Carnivores take note! This is one of the few specialist meat restaurants in Venice, with good reason, as it is run by a family of butchers. Excellent food in generous portions.

Ghetto
I Quattro Rusteghi C2 – *Campo di Ghetto Nuovo, Cannaregio 2888.*

041 715 160. Although global warming has not (yet) brought crocodiles to the Grand Canal, they have appeared on Venetian dinner plates thanks to this restaurant serving cuisine inspired by Eastern traditions. Charming service.

Gam Gam B2 – *Fond. di Cannaregio and Sottoportego del Ghetto Vecchio, Cannaregio 1122. 041 523 1495. Closed Fri evening, Sat and Jewish holidays.* A few tables beside the canal and some more in the little street leading to the heart of the Ghetto, where you can sample a range of high-quality kosher cuisine, such as hummus, moussaka, couscous, fish with haraimi sauce, and pastries.

Bentigodi (Da Francesca) C2 – *Calle Nuove (between the Rio Terrà S. Leonardo and the Ghetto), Cannaregio 1423. 041 716 269. Closed Sun evening and Mon*. This pleasant restaurant offers a wide choice of *cichèti* and innovative pasta dishes. Good wine list.

All'Antica Mola C2 – *Fond. Ormesini (opposite the Campo di Ghetto Nuovo), Cannaregio 2800. 041 717 492.* A little interior courtyard and a dining room decorated with maritime trophies provide the setting for this very simple, popular restaurant.

Expensive
Alla Palazzina B2 – *Rio Terrà S.Leonardo, at the corner of the Ponte delle Guglie, Cannaregio 1509. 041 717 725.* This restaurant with its wood-panelled walls and hidden garden offers several fish-based tasting menus, and occupies a stunning little *palazzo*. Gondoliers like to lunch here, a sign that their trade is lucrative and the food is good.

I Frari and San Rocco
Moderate

Il Réfolo B1 – *Campiello del Piovan (set back from Campo S. Giacomo dall'Orio) - S. Croce 1459. 041 524 0016. www.dafiore.net.* A place to enjoy a pizza or a more elaborate dish on a little square bordered by a canal, but be warned that it gets very busy and it may be wise to book for an evening meal.

Al Ponte B1 – *Ponte del Megio (at the corner of Calle Larga leading to Campo S. Giacomo dall'Orio), S. Croce 1666. 041 719 777.* At the end of the "millet bridge", so-called because the area used to be occupied by millet and wheat warehouses, you will find this trattoria serving excellent fish specialities.

Capitan Uncino B1 – *Campo S.Giacomo dall'Orio, S. Croce 1501. 041 721 901. Closed Wed.* Tables on the *campo* shaded by an acacia tree. Fish and seafood specialities: try the *scampi alla buzzara* with polenta, or the grilled sea bass *(branzino)*.

🍴 **La Zucca** C1 – *Calle del Tintor, near the Ponte del Meggio, S. Croce 1762. 041 524 1570. www.lazucca.it.* A restaurant offering varied, creative cuisine at reasonable prices, which is quite a rarity for Venice. Amidst the *zucca* (pumpkin)-themed décor, you can enjoy numerous dishes renowned for their vegetable accompaniments: the artichokes, aubergines, marrows, zucchini and leeks do the lagoon's market gardeners justice, whilst the delicious desserts are a gourmet delight. The restaurant is highly regarded, so booking is advised.

Trattoria S. Tomà B3 – *Campo S.Tomà, S. Polo 2864A. 041 523 8819. Closed Tue in winter.* Tables

spill out into the *campo* and an interior courtyard. Service with a smile.

Dona Onesta B3 – *Calle Larga Foscari, where it meets the Rio de la Frescada (not far from Ca' Foscari), Dorsoduro 3922. 041 710 586.* An excellent trattoria: the *sarde in saòr* with raisins and pine nuts are exemplary and the grilled fish (sea bass, sole…) is remarkable. Diligent, friendly service.

La Patatina C2 – *Calle del Saoneri - S. Polo 2741. 041 523 7238. www.lapatatina.it (in Italian).* A nice, lively, traditional restaurant offering a vast choice of very hearty dishes (often based on potatoes, as the name suggests), to eat at the bar or sitting peacefully in the company of the ever-hungry crowd of students from the nearby Ca' Foscari, or local employees.

Expensive

Antica Besseta B1 – *Salizada de Ca' Zusto, S. Croce 1395. 041 524 0428. www.anticabesseta.it (in Italian). Closed Tue and Wed lunchtime.* Traditional Venetian cuisine. A few tables in the street under a pleasant climbing vine.

Da Ignazio C2 – *Calle dei Saoneri, S. Polo 2749. 041 523 4852. www.trattoriadaignazio.com (in Italian). Closed Sat.* This elegant little restaurant with nicely dressed tables offers excellent fish specialities. Good wine list.

I Carmini
Inexpensive

Osteria ai Pugni C1 – *Ponte dei Pugni, Dorsoduro 2836.* A nice, simple little place to drink an *ómbra* and nibble on a *cichèto*.

Da Toni B1 – *Fond. S.Basilio, Dorsoduro 1642.* Beside the *rio*, a stone's throw from the church of S. Sebastiano and the port, you can join local workers tucking into the tasty home-made pasta.

Moderate

Casin dei Nobili C1 – *Calle Casin dei Nobili (facing Campo S. Barnaba), Dorsoduro 2765. 041 241 1841. Closed Mon*. The kind of place where Venetian noblemen would have consorted with women of easy virtue, although the atmosphere these days is much less racy. The restaurant, with its little dining room and a courtyard separated from the street by a wall, offers grilled meats, pasta and dishes of the day.

Pane, Vino e San Daniele A1 – *Campo dell'Anzolo Rafael, Dorsoduro 1722. 041 522 7456. www.panevinoesandaniele.net. Closed Wed*. A place devoted to the famous *prosciutto crudo*, which you can enjoy as it comes with a glass of wine or prepared with bread *gnocchi* or pasta. Friendly service and an adjoining shop.

Expensive

Ristoteca Oniga C1 – *Campo S. Barnaba, Dorsoduro 2852. 041 522 4410. www.oniga.it. Closed Tue*. This restaurant-cum-wine bar is popular amongst local artists and offers carefully prepared traditional Venetian cuisine (delicious polenta with *seppie in nero* or salt cod), as well as more innovative creations such sea bass *in crosta* served with a grape risotto.

Giudecca
Moderate

🐟 **Altanella** C1 – *Calle delle Erbe, Giudecca 268. 041 522 7780. Closed Mon and Tue*. On fine days,

the dining room of this discreet trattoria opens out onto the Rio del Ponte Lungo by way of a vine-shaded terrace. Very popular with locals, as well as anyone with a taste for true Venetian cuisine.

Luxury

Harry's Dolci B1 – *Riva San Biagio, Giudecca 773. 041 522 4844. www.cipriani.com*. On the way to the Molino Stucky, you will find this off-shoot of the legendary Harry's Bar in Calle Vallaresso.
The restaurant boasts an attractive dining room with white-tiled walls and a ceiling with exposed beams. You can sample the inventive cuisine thanks to two daily set meals, whilst the terrace on the *riva* offers a magnificent view.

Bauers Palladio D1 – *Fond. delle Zitelle, by the church of the same name, Giudecca 33. 041 520 7022. www.bauerhotels.com*. Even if you decide not to stay in this annex of the famous hotel, which is housed in the chiesa delle Zitelle's former convent school for girls, you can still enjoy snacks at lunchtime in the garden behind the building, or barbecue dishes in the evening.

Sant'Elena and San Pietro
Moderate

Giorgione A2 – *Via Garibaldi, Castello 1533. 041 522 8727*. A place serving honest local cuisine, with musical entertainment some-times provided by a singer with a guitar. Amiable, speedy service.

Dal Pampo (S. Elena) C3 – *Calle Chinotto, Castello 24. 041 520 8419. Closed Tue*. A few tables in the street in the residential district of Sant'Elena. The sight of the owners sorting through porcini mushrooms gathered from the nearby forests on one of the tables in the little dining room sums up the family atmosphere of this welcoming place, which is an unexpected treat.

Dai Tosi Grandi B2 – *Secco Marina, Castello 985. 041 520 4182. Closed Mon*. The success of this trattoria-pizzeria right by the Biennale has brought expansion and the addition of a nice little garden.

Expensive

Il Nuovo Galeon B2 – *Via Garibaldi, Castello 1308. 041 520 4656. Closed Tue*. On the corner of the *viale* leading to the Giardini Pubblici, this elegant place is one of the city's high-quality restaurants.

Luxury

Hostaria da Franz B2 – *Fond. S.Giuseppe, Castello 754. 041 522 0861. www.hostariadafranz.com*. An attractive dining room, classy surroundings and a terrace on the canal looking out on to the *campo*. With the Biennale not far away, da Franz sets out to create a sufficiently sophisticated atmosphere to attract the art world and its entourage.

Il Lido
Moderate

Andri – *Via Lepanto 21. 041 526 5482. Closed Tue*. A restaurant set in an amazing villa with a lovely carved stone loggia. The terrace is set under a genuine miniature virgin forest. Very reasonable menu based on fish and seafood.

La Sfera – *Via Lepanto, on the corner of Via Enrico Dandolo. 041 526 1722*. A place serving up the classics of Venetian cuisine in a canalside location.

Certosa

Ristorante Il Certosino – *Venice Certosa Hotel Polo Nautico Vento di Venezia. 041 520 0035. Closed Mon. Weekdays dinner only; also lunch Sat-Sun*. (*Vaporetto* 41/42 toward Murano, stop is by request, so ask the attendant when you board.) A lovely evening out begins when you step off the *vaporetto*, walk down the wooden pier, enter the boatyard where craftsmen are restoring antique boats, and settle in for a delicious meal on the patio in the garden or in this simply decorated restaurant. Fish and local vegetables dominate the summer menu, but as winter approaches, he adds hearty mountain favourites of meat, mushrooms, cheeses and other fare. Limited but good wine selection. Don't worry about the return trip in the evening, just book the complimentary water taxi.

Murano
Expensive

Ai Frati – *Fond. Venier 4. 041 736 694 - lunchtimes only, closed Thu*. For those in search of a simple *trattoria* serving seafood dishes.

Busa alla Torre – *Campo S.Stefano 3. 041 739 662. Closed evenings, except Fri-Sun and in summer*. A *trattoria* occupying a red building with a loggia. Tables are laid out in the quiet *campo*, away from the bustle of the dock.

Burano

😊 **A bit of advice** – There is a string of restaurants and *trattorie* on either side of Via Baldassare Galuppi. Some can be invaded by groups, especially in summer: so if you arrive in the morning, it would be a good idea to book a table when you get there. The *vaporetto*

(41/42) runs in the evening, so to avoid the crush linger for the sunset and have an early dinner.

Expensive

Da Romano – *Via Baldassare Galuppi, Burano 221. 041 730 030. www.daromano.it. Closed Sun evening and Tue*. In the birthplace of a proud local sailor, Giovanni Tomadelli (1861–1926), this traditional restaurant was a haven for artists, who sometimes paid their tabs with works of art. They still maintain good quality, in spite of the influx of tourists.

Al Gatto Nero - da Ruggero – *Fond. de la Giudecca, Burano 88. 041 730 120. Closed Mon*. In a peaceful canalside location, away from the crowds. This was very "in" for seafood specialities, but recently locals complain that the prices have gone up while quality teeters a bit up and down.

Torcello
Expensive

🍴 **Al Ponte del Diavolo** – *Fond. dei Borgognoni 10/11. 041 730 401. www.osteriaponte deldiavolo.com. Closed Mon*. A restaurant boasting a very pretty veranda with rattan chairs and a "gazebo" in the heart of the magnificent garden. It is only open at lunchtime, and the menu leans heavily on seafood (tuna tartare with capers, *tagliolini* with cuttlefish ink and marinated *scampi*, baked *branzino* (sea bass), or thinly sliced tuna with sauce and rosemary). A favourite, also, of other restaurateurs.

Luxury
Locanda Cipriani – *Piazza Santa Fosca 29. 041 730 150.*

www.locandacipriani.com. Closed Tue. Hemingway's former bolt-hole right by the abbey is seductively calm and authentic, and the refined cuisine is a delight.

Mazzorbo
Moderate

Maddalena – *Mazzorbo 7C, by the canal, at the LN vaporetto stop, or on foot from the Burano landing stage, following the shoreline and crossing a wooden bridge. 041 730 151. Closed Thu*. Charming Raffaella and Beppino have run this trattoria for more than 50 years. This large orange villa has a slightly wild-looking garden beside the canal that produces one of the best salads you'll ever taste.

Expensive
Venissa Ostello – *Fondamenta Santa Caterina 3. 041 527 2281. www.venissa.it Closed Nov–Mar*. The restaurant sits next to a vineyard with lovely outdoor seating and attentive service. Don't worry about lingering over dinner, Venissa's complimentary water taxi will take you back, perhaps in a lovely vintage wooden boat.

Chioggia
Moderate

El Fontego – *Piazzetta XX Settembre 497. 041 550 0953. Closed Mon*. A pizzeria and fish restaurant.

Pellestrina
Moderate

Da Celeste – *Via Vianelli 625B. 041 967 043. Closed Wed*. Fish lovers will be in their element in this restaurant decorated with modern paintings and boasting a large terrace looking out onto the lagoon.

HOTELS

Although Venice has a wide range of accommodation, visitors should be aware that prices can be high and value for money difficult to find. Venice is now a travel destination throughout the year but low season and high season prices do apply. The summer period used to be less popular (and therefore cheaper) on account of the hot, damp climate; but now that air conditioning is prevalent and the Biennale opens odd years in June, that is no longer true. Book as far in advance as possible, especially for dates during Carnival. The official tourist board has accommodation information on their website, www.turismovenezia.it. The red Michelin Guide Italy, updated yearly, provides a detailed list of recommended Venice hotels and restaurants.

Luxury	<260€	*Moderate*	100€–180€
Expensive	180–260€	*Inexpensive*	>100€

Our Selection

Our price categories are for a double room in high season. Given the significant seasonal variations, this classification is based on average prices and to help compare pricing among different hotels. Most prices quoted include breakfast. You are strongly advised to enquire beforehand and to check the rates that apply to your stay. In the summer, visitors are advised to verify that lodgings have air conditioning (especially for the basic or inexpensive premises).

☺ **A bit of advice** – The **Michelin Guide Italia** is updated every year and includes a very wide selection of hotels and restaurants.

Venice Hotel Tax

In Summer 2011, Venice initiated a tourist tax for hotel rooms, like that launched earlier in the year for the cities of Rome and Florence. The fee is per person, not per room. The tax will vary according to the category of hotel, its neighborhood, and whether the tourist season is high or low. The tourist tax regulations identify three territorial areas and two periods (high season and "other"). The territorial areas are: Venice historic centre, Giudecca and the islands dedicated mainly to accommodation (e.g. San Clemente); islands of the Venetian Lagoon (e.g. Lido, Murano, Burano, etc.); and mainland. In 2012, the total days considered high season are 257 days. Keep in mind that in summer during even years, when the Biennale is not on, there may be some good discounts toward late July and August, even if the tax rates are for high season. Overall, these distinctions can be helpful if you want to avoid crowds or to find lower hotel rates. Here are the periods of high season:
1) 1 Jan–Sun after 6 Jan; 2) the period of Carnival; 3) the first Wed before Easter–following Tuesday; 4) 1 Apr–31 Oct; 5) the week that includes the 8 December; 6) 23–31 Dec.

Choosing Your Area

Wherever you end up in Venice, you should enjoy quiet nights. The neighbourhood atmosphere varies by districts within the *sestieri*. If you like to laze in the sunshine on a café on the square, then opt for an area around a *campo* like **Santo Stefano** or, on the other side of the Grand Canal, **Santa Margherita** or **San Giacomo dall'Orio**. If you fancy an old-fashioned, slightly melancholy charm, then opt for the *sestiere* of **Dorsoduro**, between San Barnaba and La Salute. And if you thrive on hustle and bustle from the moment you get up, then try the **Riva degli Schiavoni**, the area around **St Mark's Square** or the **Rialto**, or around the **Strada Nuova**.

Hotels

Traditional hotels, known as *alberghi*, are located throughout the city. Prices vary according to location, comfort levels and views. **A bit of advice** – Don't rely exclusively on the number of stars to determine a hotel's quality.

Pensioni, Locande and Affitacamere

Generally, these are more informal than traditional hotels and often occupy a single floor of a building. With a small number of rooms, these places have the feel of a family hotel or guesthouse and can often be quite classy. Generally

you will pay less in these types of establishments than in the hotels.

Bed and Breakfasts

There are numerous bed and breakfast establishments in Venice, in all categories and all prices. As with hotels, you will have to eat lunch and dinner out.
www.interhome.fr
www.bbbv.it
www.bbitalia.it

Apartments

The rental market is well developed in Venice. For those staying several days, an apartment allows you to play at being a Venetian and to save money on meals.
Venice Apartments – *347-329-5511 (US), 020 8133 4030 (UK).*
www.veniceapartments.org.

Religious Institutions

Institutions run by religious orders providing tourist accommodation often at attractive prices. Some of them run genuine *case per ferie* offering accommodation of a standard comparable to a small hotel. Usually the atmosphere is spartan (often with no air conditioning) though invariably

© Hotel Concordia

Hotel Concordia

spotlessly clean. Note that few of these places accept credit cards, some impose a curfew and some are only open during the main visitor season, July–September. Also, some may require the occupant to vacate the premises for a certain number of hours during the day.

Youth Hostel

Venice's youth hostel boasts a superb canalside location on the island of Giudecca. It belongs to Hostelling International and is only open to holders of annual youth hostel membership. Accommodation in single-sex dormitories.

FUAJ – *27 r. Pajol - 75008 Paris - 01 44 89 87 27. www.fuaj.org.*

Campsites

Venice has no campsites in the city, but many sites along the coastline are accessible by *vaporetto*, offering accommodation in tents or furnished bungalows. A few campsites are in the Marghera-Mestre-Tessera area, as well as a site on the **Lido**, near San Nicolò (*www.campingsannicolo.com*).

Grand Canal

A bit of advice – The best rooms in certain hotels have views of the Grand Canal. Our listings here follow the route of the canal from north to south.

Left bank

Ovidius and **Sturion** – *See Rialto.*

Right bank

Ca' Nigra – *See I Frari and San Rocco.*
San Cassiano and **Rialto** – *See Rialto.*

Palazzo Sant'Angelo sul Canal Grande – *See Around La Fenice.*
Pensione Accademia "Villa Maravege" – *See Accademia.*

Piazza San Marco
Inexpensive

Ai Do Mori A2 – *Calle Larga, S.Marco 658. 041 520 8177. www.hotelaidomori.com. 11 rooms.* This friendly, intimate hotel, just steps from San Marco, is simply furnished in a very lively neighbourhood and offers reasonable rates.

Foresteria Valdese B1 – *Palazzo Cavagnis, at the end of Calle Lunga S. Maria Formosa, Castello 5170. 041 528 6797. www.foresteriavenezia.it. Various price bands.* This institution, run by the Union of Waldesian and Methodist Churches, occupies an attractive *palazzo* beside the Rio S. Severo, next to SS. Giovanni e Paolo.

Istituto San Giuseppe A1 – *Ponte della Guerra (behind S. Zulian), Castello 5402. 041 522 5352.* The institution is housed in an attractive *p* just beyond the Rio coming from San Zulian. A very nice place to stay, five minutes from St Mark's Square, with huge air-conditioned rooms.

Expensive

San Marco A2 – *Calle dei Fabbri - S.Marco 877. 041 520 4277. www.sanmarcohotels.com. 56 rooms.* Comfortable and couldn't be closer to St Mark's Square, if lacking a little in charm.

Paganelli B2 – *Riva degli Schiavoni, Castello 4182. 041 522 4324. www.hotelpaganelli.com. 22 rooms.* A family place facing St Mark's basin. A few rooms at the front benefit from the view.

©Hotel Paganelli
Paganelli

Villa Igea B2 – *Campo S. Zaccaria, Castello 4684. 041 241 0956. www. hotelvillaigea.it. 29 rooms*. ☂. This remarkably well-located annex of the Hotel Savoia e Jolanda offers well-kept rooms, some facing the church of S. Zaccaria.

Ca' dei Conti B1 – *Fond. di Remedio (a stone's throw from S. Maria Formosa), Castello 4429. 041 277 0500. www.cadeiconti.com. 15 rooms*. ☂. A harmonious façade on the corner of a romantic canal spanned by little bridges. Very comfortable rooms furnished in the 18C style, and a *cortile* (courtyard) for breakfast.

Luxury

Concordia A1 – *Calle Larga S.Marco, S. Marco 367. 041 520 6866. www.hotelconcordia.com. 55 rooms*. ☂. Very close to St Mark's Square: even though the entrance to the hotel is at the rear, some of the rooms face onto the Piazzetta dei Leoncini and offer wonderful views of the basilica and the *campanile*.

Metropole B2 – *Riva degli Schiavoni, Castello 4149. 041 520 6044. www.hotelmetropole.com. 69 rooms*. ☂. Facing St Mark's

Basin, the plush ambience successfully blends Venetian elegance with Eastern exoticism. Sgra Gloria runs a fine hotel with attentive service. Her family's antique clocks are on display throughout, as are her grandmother's antique fans, which must have fluttered through fascinating scenes. MET Restaurant, one of the city's best, merits a visit for the chef's creative cuisine, fine service and tranquil atmosphere.

Savoia e Jolanda B2 – *Riva degli Schiavoni, Castello 4187. 041 520 6644. www.hotelsavoiajolanda.com 51 rooms*. ☂. This pleasant hotel overlooking St Mark's Basin has a restaurant with terrace dining on the Riva in good weather.

🏨 **Palazzo Priuli** B1 – *Fond. dell'Osmarin, Castello 4979. 041 277 0834. www.hotelpriuli.com. 10 rooms*. ☂. Commissioned in the 14C by Antonio Priuli, of a dynasty that produced many doges, procurators and cardinals, this *palazzo* stands at the junction of two *rii*, and boasts a fine stone staircase and a large hall with a beamed ceiling on the *piano nobile*. Each room has been decorated in its own unique fashion.

Hotel Danieli
©Hotel Danieli

🛏 Danieli B2 – *Riva degli Schiavoni, Castello 4196. 041 522 6480. www.starwoodhotels.com/ danieli . 225 rooms.* 🛏. For many people, Venice is a dreamlike city in which images from literature and film merge in an unreal, decadent atmosphere. Palazzo Dandolo, home to the Hotel Danieli since 1822, suggests this dream world. Columns, banisters, galleries and intricate stonework form the incredible décor that seduced Dickens, Wagner, Balzac, Proust and Sand.

Rialto
Expensive
Left bank

Rialto B2 – *Riva del Ferro - S. Marco 5149. 041 520 9166. www.rialtohotel.com. 79 rooms.* 🛏. Just by the *vaporetto* landing stage. As you can imagine, the view over the Grand Canal and the bridge is sublime. Lots of groups.

Right bank

Sturion B2 – *Calle del Sturion, S.Polo 679. 041 523 6243. www. locandasturion.com. 11 rooms.* 🛏.
Ovidius B2 – *Calle del Sturion, S. Polo 678A. 041 523 7970. www.hotellocandaovidius.com. 15 rooms.* 🛏. These two hotels occupy two floors of the same building facing onto the Grand Canal, south of the Rialto Bridge. Besides the exceptional view, the very pleasant service makes staying in either hotel a delight.
San Cassiano (Ca' Favretto) A1 – *Calle della Rosa, S. Croce 2232. 041 524 1768. www.sancassiano.it. 36 rooms.* 🛏. A period residence set in an ancient *palazzo* faces onto the Grand Canal, opposite the Ca' d'Oro: each room is different,

and the room overlooking the Grand Canal on the *piano nobile* is exceptionally charming.

La Fenice
Moderate

Locanda San Samuele A1 – *Salizada S. Samuele (the street leading from the vaporetto stop of the same name), S. Marco 3358, upstairs at the end of the courtyard. 041 522 8045. www.albergosansamuele.it. 10 rooms (some without bathrooms).* This pretty little guesthouse gives you an excellent idea of traditional Venetian living.
Locanda Fiorita B1 – *Campiello Novo (o delle Morti), S. Marco 3457A. 041 523 4754. www. locandafiorita.com. 10 rooms.* 🛏. A welcoming guesthouse offering comfortable, charming rooms in a little *campiello* that looks like something straight out of the *commedia dell'arte*.
Domus Ciliota A1 – *Calle delle Muneghe (from the campo via Calle delle Botteghe), S. Marco 2976. 041 520 4888. www.ciliota.it. 51 rooms.* The former Augustinian monastery, founded in 1448 and renovated in 1999, is near Campo S. Stefano and Palazzo Grassi. All the institute's rooms have a shower, television, minibar, air conditioning, and you can even pay by credit card.
Locanda Art Decò AB1– *Calle delle Botteghe (opposite the church of S. Stefano), S. Marco 2966. 041 277 0558. www.locandaartdeco. com. 6 rooms.* You'll love this tiny but magnificently located and furnished *locanda*; the attic room is lovely, although taller guests risk knocking themselves out on a ceiling beam!

Expensive

Serenissima C1 – *Calle Goldoni (a stone's throw from Campo S. Luca), S. Marco 4486. 041 520 0011. www.hotelserenissima.it. 37 rooms.* ⌲. This simple, pleasant hotel is very close to St Mark's Square and offers rooms decorated with modern paintings.

Palazzo del Giglio B1 – *Campo S. Maria del Giglio, S. Marco 2462. 041 271 9111. www.hotelgiglio.com.* ⌲. The sienna-coloured terrace and green shutters lend this hotel facing onto the *campo* a certain character. Very comfortable with an excellent location right by the *vaporetto*.

Luxury

Kette B1 – *Piscina San Moisè, S.Marco 2053. 041 520 7766. www.hotelkette.com. 63 rooms.* ⌲. The hotel is set in an evocative 16C residence, right by La Fenice, on the corner of a street that leads only to the Rio dei Barcaroli, so peace and quiet are guaranteed.

🏨 **Gritti Palace** B1 – *Campo S. Maria del Giglio, S. Marco 2467. 041 794 611. www.starwoodhotels.com/ grittipalace. 85 rooms.* To really "live like a doge", try this former home to Doge Andrea Gritti, a *palazzo* that conjures images of film stars, alighted for the Film Festival, posing on the hotel's terrace. Gritti seems to float on the Grand Canal, with La Salute in the background. As for the interior, the pride that the Gritti Palace puts into preserving the city's charms can be seen in every detail.

Flora B1 – *Calle dei Bergamaschi (to the left of the Calle Larga 22 Marzo), S. Marco 2283A. 041 520 5844. www.hotelflora.it - 44 rooms*

- ⌲. A remarkably well-located hotel right by St Mark's Square and La Fenice, in a small *palazzo* at the end of a quiet street, with a nice flower-filled garden where you can have breakfast.

Santo Stefano A1 – *Campo S. Stefano, S. Marco 2957. 041 520 0166. www.hotelsantostefano venezia.com. 11rooms.* ⌲. A discreet hotel set in a tall building, with rooms all facing onto the *campo* and catching the morning sun. You can take your breakfast outside the hotel, with plants to shield you from the gaze of passers-by.

Palazzo Sant'Angelo sul Canal Grande A1 – *Ramo del Teatro de S. Angelo, S. Marco 3878B. 041 241 1452. www.sinahotels.com. 26 rooms.* ⌲. This superb *palazzo* with its private landing stage on the Grand Canal offers huge rooms and bathrooms equipped with whirlpool baths, some of them facing out onto the prestigious Grand Canal.

Accademia
Moderate

Ca' San Trovaso A1 – *Fond. delle Eremite (access via the no-through-road), Dorsoduro 1351. 041 277 1146. www.casantrovaso.com* ⌲. Beside the Rio delle Eremite, in other words behind the church of S. Trovàso, you will find this inexpensive hotel (by Venetian standards, at least) in a district noted for its melancholy charm.

Expensive

Pensione Accademia "Villa Maravege" B1 – *Fond. Bollani, Dorsoduro 1058. 041 521 0188. www.pensioneaccademia.it. 27 rooms.* This fine Neoclassical residence is fronted by an attractive statue-filled garden at the meeting of the Rio della Toletta and the Rio S. Tròvaso, and makes for a charming place to stay.

Agli Alboretti B1 – *Rio Terrà Antonio Foscarini, Dorsoduro 884. 041 523 0058. www.aglialboretti. com. 23 rooms.* 🖵. One of the nicest hotels you will find, with a garden shaded by an arbour, and welcoming staff. Very comfortable.

Belle Arti B1 – *Rio Terrà Antonio Foscarini, Dorsoduro 912A. 041 522 6230. www.hotelbellearti.com.* 🖵. A very pretty garden with a fountain surrounded by a covered gallery adds to the appeal of this comfortable hotel.

Luxury

Ca' Pisani B1 – *Rio Terrà Antonio Foscarini, Dorsoduro 979A. 041 240 1411. www.capisanihotel.it. 29 rooms.* 🖵. Class and refinement with the Ponte dell'Accademia on your doorstep. Rooms have various themes, from the plush red brocade Doge's room to Marco Polo's Oriental room.

La Salute
Inexpensive

Istituto Suore Salesie B1 – *Rio Terrà dei Catecumeni, Dorsoduro 108. 041 522 3691. 24 rooms (shared bathrooms).* 🖵. A large building in the quiet district between the basilica and the Giudecca Canal.

Moderate

Messner A1 – *Rio Terrà dei Catecumeni, near the Fond. Ca' Balà, Dorsoduro 216. 041 522 7443. www.hotelmessner.it. 13 rooms.* 🖵. Fairly similar to **Istituto Suore Salesie**, but without its view of the *rio*.

Zattere

Pensione La Calcina A1 – *Zattere ai Gesuati, Dorsoduro 780. 041 520 6466. www.lacalcina.com. 27 rooms.* 🖵. Only a photograph in the entrance hall remains of the *locanda* where Ruskin stayed in 1876. A restoration has re-created its former appearance, rooms furnished with simple early 20C furniture and hardwood floors. The hotel boasts a wonderful location on the Giudecca Canal. Its restaurant, La Piscina, has good food, reasonable prices, and terrace tables on the Giudecca Canal.

Luxury

American Dinesen A1 – *Fond. Bragadin (San Vio), Dorsoduro 628. 041 520 4733. www.hotel american.com. 30 rooms.* 🖵. This was the area where Venice's American expats used to gather, including Ezra Pound, who lived on the nearby Fondamenta Ca'Bala. With its flower-bedecked windows, this comfortable hotel will satisfy the most demanding of guests.

Schiavoni and Arsenale
Luxury

Liassidi Palace A2 – *Calle della Madonna/Ponte dei Greci, Castello 3405. 041 520 5658. www.liassidipalacehotel.com. 26 rooms.* 🖵. A large courtyard stands in front of this refined 18C *palazzo*. A very comfortable choice, with an excursion to Murano included in the price.

Santi Giovanni e Paolo
Expensive

Locanda SS. Giovanni e Paolo C3 – *Calle Ospedaleto (on the right-hand side of Barbaria delle Tolle, just after the church), Castello*

6401. 041 522 2767. *www.locanda
ssgiovannipaolo.it*. 🛏. *Closed
Nov.* A modest *locanda* but well
located close to the statue of the
Condottiere Colleoni.

Locanda Ca' La Corte B3 –
*Calle Bressana, on the corner of
Fond. dei Felzi, Castello 6317. 041
241 1300. www.locandalacorte.it.
16 rooms.* 🛏. A charming hotel
with floral window displays,
occupying an attractive 16C
residence facing onto the Rio S.
Giovanni Laterano. A *Cortile* and
tasteful interiors complete the
picture.

Ca' d'Oro A2 – *Corte Barbaro
(via the Salizada del Tentor from
Campo SS. Apostoli), Cannaregio
4604. 041 241 1212. www.venice
hotelcadoro.com. 27 rooms.* 🛏.
The rooms of this pleasant little
hotel are arranged around a *corte*
with access to the Rio di Ca' d'Oro
via a *sottoportego*.

Giorgione A2 – *Salizada del Pistor/
Calle Larga dei Proverbi (at the
corner of Campo di SS. Apostoli),
Cannaregio 4587. 041 522 5810.
www.hotelgiorgione.com. 76
rooms.* 🛏. This hotel occupying a
whole block encloses a nice flower-
filled garden with a fountain, away
from the bustle of the *campo*.

Ca' d'Oro
Inexpensive
Casa Studentesca Santa Fosca
A2 – *Fond. Fra Daniele Canal (via
Campo S. Fosca and the bridge
over the rio of the same name),
Cannaregio 2372. 041 715 775.
www.santafosca.it. 57 rooms.*
At the end of an extremely tranquil
fondamenta, but not far from the
Strada Nuova, this university hall
of residence offering spartan
accommodation is located in a

former convent. There is a curfew -
be back by midnight.

Casa Cardinal Piazza B2 –
*Fond. Gasparo Contarini,
Dorsoduro 3539A. 041 721 388.
24 rooms.* An institution offering
sober hospitality on the canalside
walkway leading from the
Madonna dell'Orto to the Sacra
della Misericordia.

Luxury
Ai Mori d'Oriente A2 – *Fond.
della Sensa, Cannaregio 3319.
041 711 001. www.morihotel.com.
61 rooms.* 🛏. With a bar facing
onto the quiet *rio*, this newcomer
features Moorish décor in this 15C
palazzo, sure to satisfy discerning
guests.

**Boscolo Venezia (formerly
Grand Hotel dei Dogi)** A2 – *Fond.
Madonna dell'Orto, Cannaregio
3500. 041 220 8111. www.boscolo
hotels.com. 71 rooms.* 🛏.
This out-of-the-way district
makes an unusual setting for this
kind of luxury hotel. The most
extraordinary thing about this 17C
palazzo, however, is the huge park
leading down to the lagoon and its
private landing stage. A place for
well-heeled guests in search of
the quiet life.

Ca' Sagredo B3 – *Campo S.Sofia,
Ca' d'Oro, Cannaregio 4198/99.
041 241 3111. www.casagredo
hotel.com. 42 rooms.* 🛏. This
marvellous 13C *palazzo* is named
after the last Venetian aristocratic
family to own the building, who
took it over in the 18C. You'll
be amazed by Andrea Tirali's
monumental staircase, Pietro
Longhi's immense fresco of the *Fall
of the Giants*, the *portego* decorated
with paintings by Andrea Urbani,
the music room adorned with

gilding and mythological frescoes by Gaspare Diziani, and the Tiepolo room, a tribute to the city painted by the artist.

Cannaregio and the Ghetto
Moderate

Ca' San Marcuola C3 – *Campo S. Marcuola (from the Strada Nuova via the Rio Terrà del Cristo), Cannaregio 1763. 041 716 048. www.casanmarcuola.com.* ⌁. This renovated hotel comes equipped with a lift and is located close to the *vaporetto* stop of the same name, making it a very acceptable choice.

Abbazia B3 – *Calle Priuli dei Cavaletti, Cannaregio 68. 041 717 333. www.abbaziahotel.com. 39 rooms.* ⌁. Part of the Barefoot Carmelites' monastery, the tranquil atmosphere and rigorous elegance make this hotel a lovely stay close to the station. The refectory, with its benches and pulpit, is used as a bar, and the cloister garden is a perfect place to read, paint, or sip a drink.

Ca' Dogaressa B2 – *Fond. di Cannaregio (access via the Calle del Sottoportego Oscuro) 1018. 041 275 9441. www.cadogaressa.com. 6 rooms.* ⌁. The soberly decorated rooms in this little hotel are well equipped, adorned with painted furniture in the Venetian style, as well as very pleasant bathrooms. The hotel also has a terrace, and breakfast is served beside the canal when the weather is good.

Tre Archi A2 – *Fond. di Cannaregio 923. 041 524 4356. www.hoteltrearchi.com. 24 rooms.* ⌁. This hotel with rooms decorated in the local style occupies a lovely *palazzo*

overlooking the canal. As a further bonus, the flower-filled garden is an example of the sort of secret garden you can find in the city.

Ghetto

Locanda del Ghetto C2 – *Campo di Ghetto Nuovo, Cannaregio 2892. 041 275 9292. www.locanda delghetto.net. 8 rooms.* ⌁. This former synagogue constitutes the Ghetto's only accommodation option: a comfortable little *locanda* offering kosher breakfasts.

Luxury

Bellini B3 – *Lista di Spagna, Cannaregio 116A. 041 524 2488. www.boscolohotels.com. 87 rooms.* ⌁. The rooms of this hotel are all very different, ranging from the very sober to the almost sumptuous. Some have views onto the Grand Canal. A high-end hotel on the road to the station boasting refined décor and impeccable service.

I Frari and San Rocco
Inexpensive

Casa Caburlotto A3 – *Fond. Rizzi, S. Croce 316/318. 041 710 877. 45 rooms.* A university hall of residence open all year round, offering simple, comfortable rooms in a peaceful area of S. Croce, beyond the Rio Nuovo. Curfew at 10.35pm.

Domus Civica A2 – *Calle Sacchere (near the Rio delle Muneghette, close to S. Rocco), S. Polo 3082. 041 721 103. www.domuscivica. com (in Italian). 71 rooms.* This university residence for young women considered to be deserving of assistance offers very plainly decorated rooms. Shared toilets and showers.

MUST STAY

Ca' Foscari B3 – *Calle de la Frescada (continuation of Calle Lunga Foscari), Dorsoduro 3887B. 041 710 401. www.locandaca foscari.com. 11rooms (some without bathrooms)*. 🖵.
Extremely simple but well located right by the *campo*, this *locanda* is one of the city's few bargain accommodation options.

Moderate

Casa Rezzonico A3 – *Fond. Gherardini, Dorsoduro 2813. 041 277 0653. www.casarezzonico.it. 6rooms*. 🖵. Renovated rooms, some of them facing onto the *rio*, a garden where you can breakfast in the sunshine and a *campo* on your doorstep.

Gardena A1 – *Fond. dei Tolentini, S. Croce 239. 041 220 5000. www.gardenahotels.it. 19 rooms*. 🖵. This extremely comfortable hotel beside an attractive canal has been renovated and decorated with murals.

Falier A2 – *Salizada S. Pantalon - S. Croce 130. 041 710 882. www. hotelfalier.com. 19 rooms*. 🖵. A good choice for those in search of a peaceful stay, close to Campo S. Margherita and the church of S. Pantalòn.

Expensive

Ai Due Fanali B1 – *Campo S. Simeone Grande. S. Croce 946. 041 718 490. www.aiduefanali.com. 16 rooms*. 🖵. Occupying the former Scuola S. Simeone, this little hotel on a quiet *campo* facing onto the Grand Canal is notable for its peaceful atmosphere as well as its refinement. You can also enquire here about renting apartments overlooking St Mark's Basin.

Locanda San Barnaba B3 – *Calle del Traghetto, Dorsoduro 2785-2786. 041 241 1233. www.locanda-sanbarnaba.com. 13 rooms*. 🖵. A stone's throw from the Ca' Rezzonico *vaporetto*, this discreet but pleasant choice occupies a 16C *palazzo* with a nice *cortile*.

Al Sole A2 – *Fond. Minotto - S.Croce 134/136. 041 244 0328. www.alsolehotels.com. 51 rooms*. 🖵. A hotel set in a fine old *palazzo* with a façade featuring an attractive loggia. Some of the rooms have views over the garden, whilst others face the *rio*. In the attractive bar, the exposed beams of the ceiling are supported by columns adorned with capitals, and the hotel is also equipped with a lift, which is quite a rarity in the city of the doges.

Luxury

Ca' Nigra B1 – *Campo S. Simeone Grande, S. Croce 927. 041 275 0047. www.hotelcanigra.com. 21rooms*. 🖵. You access this hotel through a lovely garden with an immaculate lawn. It was opened in 2006 in a historic *palazzo* facing onto the Grand Canal, Rio Marin and the *campo*. The luxurious interior mixes period details with contemporary design. Breakfast is served on a flower-filled terrace overlooking the Grand Canal.

I Carmini
Expensive

Tiziano A1 – *Calle Rielo (near S.Niccolò dei Mendicoli), Dorsoduro 1873. 041 275 0071. www.hoteltizianovenezia.it. 14 rooms*. 🖵. A very well-kept and welcoming hotel in an extremely quite district.

Cipriani

©Genius Loci/Orient Express

Giudecca
Inexpensive

Ostello di Venezia D1 – *Fond. delle Zitelle, Giudecca 86. 041 523 8211. www.ostellovenezia.it.* ☎. Venice's youth hostel boasts a superb location opposite the Zattere.

Luxury

Cipriani & Palazzo Vendramin D1 – *Giudecca 10. 041 520 7744. www. hotelcipriani.com. 74 rooms.* ☎. A symbol of true, made-to-measure elegance and taste, in a location away from the hordes, and with a small spa.

Sant'Elena and San Pietro
Moderate

Ca' Formenta A2 – *Via Garibaldi, Castello 1650. 041 528 5494. www.hotelcaformenta.it. 14rooms.* ☎. A charming little hotel occupying a renovated house with a façade painted ochre-pink, almost on the corner of the Riva. A good choice not too far from the centre on the edge of a working-class district.

Patronato Salesiano B2 – *Calle S.Domenico (almost at the mouth of the Rio S. Giuseppe), Castello 1281. 041 240 3611.* ☎. Well located in a very 1950s-style

residence, opposite the Island of Sant'Elena.

Expensive

Sant'Elena C3 – *Calle Buccari (at the corner of Calle del Carnaro), Castello 10. 041 271 7811. www. hotelsantelena.com. 77 rooms.* ☎. This hotel run by the Best Western chain stands in a quiet, very un-Venetian-looking district. The plus points are the peace and quiet and the comfortable surroundings of the hotel itself, but on the minus side, Sant'Elena is a long way from everything, but has a *vaporetto* stop.

Il Lido
Moderate

Atlanta Augustus – *Via Lepanto 15. 041 526 0569. www.hotel atlantaugustus.com. 38 rooms.* ☎. *Closed Dec–Jan.* A large Art Nouveau building beside a canal. The rooms on the *piano nobile* have generous balconies, and the two suites on the roof-terrace have wonderful views.

Byron – *Via Bragadin 30 (behind the Hotel des Bains, a stone's throw from Lungomare Marconi). 041 526 0052. 38 rooms.* ☎. Comfort and tranquillity in this tastefully appointed little hotel in a green residential district.

Expensive

Villa Laguna – *Via Sandro Gallo 6 (100m to the right of the vaporetto landing stage). 041 526 1316. www.hotelvilllaguna.it. 12 rooms.* ⬛. A pink villa with a pleasant garden and a location on the lagoon looking towards Venice.

Luxury

Grande Albergo Ausonia & Hungaria – *Gran Viale S. Maria Elisabetta 28. 041 242 0060. www.hungaria.it (in Italian). 80 rooms.* ⬛. An extraordinary Art Nouveau palace dating from 1905, with a façade covered in painted tiles. The hotel has been fully renovated to suggest some of the unique atmosphere of its heyday. Thai spa.

🔥 **Excelsior** – *Lungomare G. Marconi 41. 041 526 0201. www.ho10.net. 197 rooms.* With its incredible architecture, this vast hotel on the beach is a sight in itself! Since 1908, it has symbolised a certain art of appearing in public… During the Film Festival, fans camp out in front of the entrance, whilst the stars discreetly leave via the underground passage leading to the private dock and the canal heading out to the lagoon.

Chioggia
Moderate

Grande Italia – *Rione S. Andrea 597 (on Piazzetta Vigo). 041 400 515. www.hotelgrandeitalia.com. 58 rooms.* ⬛. This large, restored Belle Époque-style manor house faces onto the lagoon. A very comfortable hotel with a refined atmosphere.

Certosa
Moderate

Venice Certosa Hotel – *Isola della Certosa. 041 277 8632. www.venicecertosahotel.com. 18 rooms.* ⬛. Open year-round, situated next to Vento di Venezia boatyard where you can see historic boats being restored, this friendly informal hotel is a dream for anyone wishing to escape the crowds of San Marco, as well as for sailors and boating enthusiasts, who often dock their craft and plan excursions. Lovely outside patio with small garden to relax and plenty of land for children to run about in. Their complimentary evening taxi service makes it easy to go into the centre for dinner or a concert. But don't miss dinner here; chef Roberto Tollio, who arrived in 2011, is talented at both traditional and creative cuisine and has recently given much pizzazz to dining here.

Mazzorbo
Inexpensive to Expensive

Venissa Ostello – *Fondamenta Santa Caterina 3,- 041 527 2281. www.venissa.it. 6 rooms.* ⬛. *Closed Nov–Mar.* This small estate house on the edge of the lagoon and Venissa vineyard has two options: inexpensive rooms with shared bath, or more expensive with private bath. Try La Dorona, the estate's limited-production wine. The restaurant, in a separate building, has talented chef Paola Budel whose mastery blends local produce, tradition and interesting creative touches and well-selected wines. Enquire about Venissa's complimentary taxi service.

HOTELS

VENICE

INDEX

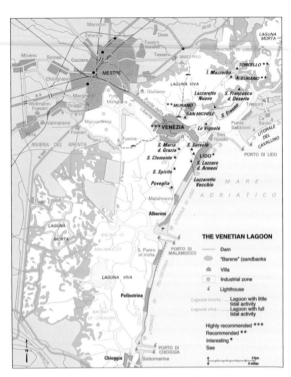

THE VENETIAN LAGOON

— Dam
"Barene" (sandbanks)
🏠 Villa
○ Industrial zone
🗼 Lighthouse

Laguna morta : ..... Lagoon with little tidal activity
Laguna viva : ..... Lagoon with full tidal activity

Highly recommended ★★★
Recommended ★★
Interesting ★
See